# MINDFULNESS & SELF-COMPASSION

## WORKBOOK FOR KIDS, VOLUME 1

# MINDFULNESS & SELF-COMPASSION

WORKBOOK FOR KIDS, VOLUME 1

40+ Fun Activities & Comics to
Learn to Self-Regulate,
Find Peace, and Be Kind to Yourself

Written by Jamie Lynn Tatera, MS
Foreword by Kristin Neff, PhD

Illustrations by Alexis Warshall
Book Design by Alyssa Brown

*Copyright © 2024 by Jamie Lynn Tatera*

*This publication is sold with the understanding that the publisher is not engaged in rendering psychological, financial, legal, or other professional services. Individual health concerns should be evaluated by a qualified professional. No warranties of any kind are declared or implied.*

*Published in the United States by Wholly Mindful, LLC.*

*Wholly Mindful and Resilience Habits are trademarks of Wholly Mindful, LLC. Milwaukee, WI.*

*All rights reserved. No part of this book may be reproduced, stored in a retrieval system or transmitted by any means–electronic, mechanical, photocopying, microfilming, recording, or otherwise–without the written consent of the author.*

*The Mindfulness and Self-Compassion Workbook for Kids has been adapted from the Mindfulness and Self-Compassion for Children and Caregivers and the Path to Resilience programs, developed by Jamie Lynn Tatera. The Mindfulness and Self-Compassion for Children and Caregivers program is an adaptation of the Mindful Self-Compassion program created by Christopher Germer and Kristin Neff, who granted permission to use the adapted material for this workbook.*

*For more information, or to book an event, visit www.jamielynntatera.com.*

*Library of Congress Cataloging-in-Publication data is available.*
*ISBN 978-1-952848-03-2 (PB)*
*Ebook ISBN 978-1-952848-04-9*

*To my little Kiwi Birds,*
Maya and Anjali.
Thank you for your patience, love and support.
And to all children….may you know how precious and wonderful you are.

**This book belongs to:**

_____

# Table of Contents

Foreword .................................................................... III
A Note to Grown-ups ........................................... IV
A Note to Kids & the Resilience Habit Animals ... VI
Quiz: What is your feelings habit animal? ............ X
Meet the Kids' Team & Create Your Avatar .......... XIII

**ADVENTURES IN FOUNDATION FOREST** ........ 1

**Adventure 1: The Land of Connection** ............ 2
Comic 1: It's Human to Have Feelings ................ 3
A Note for What to Expect on Our Adventures ... 6
Activity 1.1: Feelings Emojis ............................... 7
Activity 1.2: When Do Feelings Pop Up? ........... 8
Activity 1.3: Piano Key Feelings .......................... 9
Activity 1.4: Human, Just Like Me ....................... 11

**Adventure 2: The Land of Freedom** ............... 16
Comic 2: More than one Feeling ........................ 17
Activity 2.1: Side-by-Side Feelings .................... 20
Activity 2.2: Big and Little Feelings .................... 22
Activity 2.3: Feeling Foods ................................. 24
Activity 2.4: Share the Plate ............................... 25

**Adventure 3: The Land of Mindfulness** .......... 31
Comic 3: Notice the Now ..................................... 32
Activity 3.1: Curiosity is a Superpower .............. 35
Activity 3.2: Feel Your Feet ................................. 36
Activity 3.3: Mindful Seeing and Listening ......... 39
Activity 3.4: Puppy Dog Mind Training ............... 41

**Adventure 4: The Land of Acceptance** ........... 47
Comic 4: Ups and Downs .................................... 48
Activity 4.1: Rollercoaster of Life ........................ 51
Activity 4.2: Mixed Moments ............................... 52
Activity 4.3: Mind Muddles .................................. 53
Activity 4.4: Mind Muddle Messages .................. 56

### Adventure 5: The Land of Sensations 61
Comic 5: Does Your Body Feel Emotions? 62
Activity 5.1: X-Ray Yourself 65
Activity 5.2: Color Your Feelings 67
Activity 5.3: Squeeze and Soften 69
Activity 5.4: Stretch Like an Animal 71

### Adventure 6: The Land of Curiosity 77
Comic 6A: Hidden Emotions 78
Activity 6.1: Don't Think About the Pink Elephant! 81
Activity 6.2: What are Your Elephants? 83
Comic 6B: The Power of Naming 85
Activity 6.3: Name it to Tame it 86
Activity 6.4: Opening Up to Your Elephants 88

## ADVENTURES IN SWEET MEADOW 95

### Adventure 7: The Land of Friendship 96
Comic 7: Treat Yourself Like a Good Friend 97
Activity 7.1: How Would You Treat a Friend? 100
Activity 7.2: Being a Good Friend 102
Activity 7.3: Gentle and Strong Self-Compassion 104
Activity 7.4: When Self-Compassion Feels Awkward 106

### Adventure 8: The Land of Kindness 111
Comic 8: Kind Wishes 112
Activity 8.1: Sending Kind Wishes 115
Activity 8.2: What Do You Value? 117
Activity 8.3: Make Your Own Kindness Shirt 118
Activity 8.4: Kindness for Everyone 119

## CERTIFICATE OF COMPLETION 126

Acknowledgments 130
Resources 131
References 131

## FOREWORD BY DR. KRISTIN NEFF

Self-compassion is the foundation for resilience. In today's increasingly chaotic world, the need for children to develop self-compassion has never been greater.

I have dedicated my life to researching self-compassion and developing ways to teach it to others, including co-creating the 8-week Mindful Self-Compassion (MSC) program. Research has shown that MSC training increases well-being and decreases anxiety, depression, and a host of other challenges in adults and youths. Jamie Lynn has developed an adaptation of the MSC program for children so they can learn the vital skill of self-compassion. The activities in this series of books incorporate many of the playful ideas from her MSC adaptation along with a host of related resilience skills.

Children learn through play. These Mindfulness and Self-Compassion Workbooks for Kids make it fun and entertaining for children to learn and grow self-compassion skills. The activities are engaging, and there are delightful illustrations throughout. Additionally, there is a collection of kind characters and animal friends that model compassionate reactions to difficult feelings on their adventure, providing important resources for coping and resilience.

A core pillar of self-compassion is remembering that we are not alone in our struggles. One of the things that makes this book truly impactful is the diverse group of real children who share their strengths and struggles on the journey of self-compassion. This book is full of common humanity and connection.

There are also tips for grown-ups throughout the book. While this book can be used by a child on their own, it is best used by a child with a caregiver. When caregivers embody self-compassion and speak self-compassionately out loud, children learn that this is a healthy way to relate to oneself.

This book is a goldmine for every parent and teacher who wants to help children develop resilience and self-compassion.

Dr. Kristin Neff, PhD
Co-Founder of the Center for Mindful Self-Compassion

## A Note to Grown-Ups

Welcome! I am grateful that you are here to support children in growing resilience and self-compassion skills. Ups and downs are a part of life for everyone, and depending on how we respond to them, we either become more resilient, connected and happy, or we become more anxious, depressed and stressed. Self-compassion is a friend that we can take with us on the roller coaster of life. It can hold us close when we need a hug, and cheer us on when we need encouragement. This series of books is designed to help kids meet struggles with mindfulness and self-compassion so they can become their happiest, most resilient selves.

My name is Jamie Lynn Tatera, and I'm a parent, educator, and certified Mindful Self-Compassion teacher. I have been teaching mindfulness and self-compassion skills to children for over a decade in both the home and school environments. I have a passion for developing playful and effective programs for children, and many of the ideas from this series of books come from two of my programs: The Path to Resilience and Mindfulness and Self-Compassion for Children and Caregivers. Mindfulness and Self-Compassion for Children and Caregivers (MSC-CC) is a researched and approved parent-child adaptation of the Mindful Self-Compassion program developed by Drs. Kristin Neff and Chris Germer.

I discovered self-compassion when my sensory-sensitive, older daughter was four years old. I was trying to calm her frequent outbursts using "calming techniques," and I was having disastrous results. Fortune (and a good therapist) led me to self-compassion training, and I never looked back.

Turns out that my daughter didn't need me to help her to "be calm"; she needed me to help her feel loved, understood, and nurtured during her challenging moments. She needed to know that it was human to sometimes have big feelings, and that she was lovable even during her most difficult times. It was self-compassion that helped me show up for her in this way. First I learned to offer myself compassion for how hard it was to have a daughter that was melting down. Then I learned to offer her compassion for how hard it was to be sensory sensitive and have melt-downs.

At the time of writing this book, that four-year-old girl is a teenager who has developed the resource of self-compassion to help her through the ups and downs of life. While she still has her struggles, she knows how to love and support herself during difficult moments. Self-Compassion is a resource that I wish for every caregiver and child, and this book provides a pathway for sharing this gift with kids.

I created this series of activity books along with a team of children. We know that children learn best through play, and kids like to hear the experiences of other kids. For that reason, this book includes quotes from real kids, comics, and engaging activities. Please know that even though the ideas and activities are playful, children are learning some serious mindfulness and self-compassion skills.

You can approach this journey as a co-learner with your child. Your child may wish to do this workbook with you, or they may wish to do it on their own. Sometimes groups of parents do this workbook together so that they can learn the skills they want their child to grow.

If you read the book to your child, you might ask the child how they would like to listen - sitting still? Playing with blocks or a fidget toy? Coloring while they listen? Sometimes children feel more at ease learning self-compassion skills when they are active with their hands. Let go of doing this perfectly and enjoy the ride.

There are little notes for grown-ups throughout the book, and there are more self-compassion resources at the end of the book. Thank you for your dedication to helping kids grow mindfulness and self-compassion. I'm excited for your child (and you) to begin this journey.

*With love and deep gratitude,*
## Jamie Lynn Tatera

P.S. What kids like most about this book is the animals. There are four "feelings habit animals" featured in the quiz on pages X-XI. You can take the quiz along with your child, and share your feelings habit animal(s) with your child. On the next page, you will meet five resilience animals who will teach your kids helpful habits.

- Buddy the dog helps us know we're not alone.
- Spots the giraffe notices everything.
- Snuggles the bunny is comforting and strong.
- Doodles the dolphin helps us take action.
- Sunny always sees the good in things.

These animals can help your child playfully grow resilience habits.
Visit https://jamielynntatera.com/workbook-for-kids-resources/ for additional workbook resources.

# A Note to Kids

Hi! I'm Jamie Lynn Tatera, and I've created this series of activity books along with a team of kids. Together we have made this book as FUN and interesting as possible. Even though the comics and activities are fun, the stuff that you will be learning - mindfulness, self-compassion and growing the good - can make a BIG difference in your life. If you do all of the adventures in this series of books, you will become more resilient and self-compassionate.

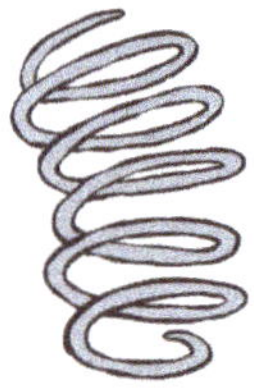

I'd like you to meet some characters that will accompany you throughout this book.

The **Resilience Habit Animals** help us learn resilience habits.

*Ummm... Owl... It's almost Doodles the dolphin's tenth birthday, and Doodles has never ever had a birthday party. I think we should throw a surprise party for Doodles.*

*That's a great idea! We can have a surprise birthday party for Doodles and make a magical cake. This scroll has all of the ingredients we need.*

## INGREDIENTS FOR OUR MAGICAL CAKE

**Foundation Forest batter ingredients***

- Eggs
- Flour
- Vanilla extract
- Baking powder
- Milk
- Butter

*Doodles is going to be so surprised and excited!*

**Sweeteners from Sweet Meadow**

- Sugar
- Chocolate Chips
- Freeze dried strawberries
- Powdered sugar
- Honey

**Magic Potion from Magic Mountains** made from....
Rainbow, gems, heart energy, gold, and sprinkles

*Allergy friendly substitutes include flax seeds, gluten-free flour, and plant-based milk and oil.

We will go on a quest to gather the ingredients, and we will use this map.

# Quiz - What is your feelings habit animal?

*Choose the option(s) that best describes how you would respond to each situation below. There is no right or wrong answer, so just choose what seems true for you. It's okay to pick more than one answer for a question.* If none of the answers fit, you can write your answer under "e" other.

1. Your friend doesn't play with you during recess. Do you…
   a. Think about it the rest of the day
   b. Get really mad or mope and feel sad
   c. Tell yourself that you don't care
   d. Think that your friend doesn't like you anymore
   e. Other _____


2. You did poorly on a test that you studied for. Do you….
   a. Keep thinking about it over and over
   b. Get really frustrated or disappointed
   c. Convince yourself that it doesn't matter
   d. Think that you're not a good student
   e. Other _____


3. Your parent yells at you because you are running late for school or for some other reason. Do you…
   a. Think about it at school
   b. Yell back at your parent or start crying
   c. Ignore your parent
   d. Tell yourself you're a bad kid
   e. Other _____

x

4. If your friend was feeling sad, would you…
   a. Keep asking them why they are sad
   b. Feel really sad because they are sad
   c. Pretend like you don't notice
   d. Wonder if you did something to make them sad
   e. Other _____

5. You feel upset and your friend or parent asks you what's wrong. Do you….
   a. Tell them detailed stories about what happened
   b. Let all your feelings come spilling out
   c. Shrug your shoulders and say you're fine
   d. Not tell them because you don't want them to feel bad, too
   e. Other _____

6. A friend or sibling is better than you at something that you have been trying hard to improve. Do you…
   a. Keep thinking about how they are better than you
   b. Feel very angry or disappointed that you can't level up
   c. Tell yourself that you don't really care about being good at the activity anyways
   d. Tell yourself that you shouldn't feel jealous
   e. Other _____

Count up the number of different letters that you chose. Whichever letters were most common for you, please know that you are not alone! However you respond to your emotions, it makes sense, and there are other kids who feel like you.

| a | b | c | d | e |
|---|---|---|---|---|
|   |   |   |   |   |

*If you'd like, you can count or tally the letters you circled.*

Below is a list of animals that match with the letters you may have chosen. You might be a combination of more than one.

 If you had **mostly a's**, your feelings habit animal is a beaver - Emotions can be sticky for you. Your mind replays situations over and over. A sticky mind can be tricky, but it can also be STRONG.

 If you had **mostly b's**, your feelings habit animal is a bear - You feel BIG feelings. It's healthy to feel our feelings, but big feelings can be hard to manage. Being sensitive can also be a gift.

 If you had **mostly c's**, your feelings habit animal is a chameleon - Sometimes your feelings hide, or you distract yourself from them. Avoiding feelings can cause problems over time, but shifting your focus can also be helpful.

 If you had **mostly d's**, your feelings habit animal is a deer - You sometimes think it's not okay to feel your feelings. Shame can make you feel bad about yourself, but caring deeply is a strength.

 If you had **mostly e's**, your feelings habit animal is a dragon - You might have a mix of different ways you respond to feelings. It's common for feeling habits to be tricky in some ways and helpful in other ways.

What is your feelings habit animal(s)? _ _ _ _ _ _ _ _ _ _ _ _ _ _ _ _ _ _ _ _ _ _ _ _ _ _ _ _

**If you'd like, you can draw your feelings habit animal(s) below:**

# Meet the Kids' Team

You will go on this adventure with <u>real kids</u> who helped to create this book! Here members of the Kids Team share a bit about themselves including their feelings habit animals.

*Circle the kids who have the same feelings habit animals as you.*

*Even though I hide my feelings, I still feel them like you.*

**Ambika:** I like reading and playing tennis.

"Sometimes I distract myself from my emotions because I don't want to feel them. I'm a little bit of all the animals, but mostly I'm a chameleon."
—Ambika, age 12

**Khalil:** I like to play soccer and baseball, and I like to play video games.

"Sometimes I blow up as a bear. I feel like I'm sort of a beaver, too."
—Khalil, age 8

**Anjali:** I am creative with my sister, and I like acting and reading.

"Sometimes I hide my feelings until I can't anymore. Then I beat myself up for having my emotions and hiding them. My feelings habit animals are a deer and a beaver."
—Anjali, age 10

**Dallas:** I like to play soccer and look at my snakes.

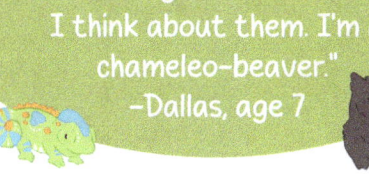

"Sometimes I hide mad and sad feelings, and sometimes I think about them. I'm a chameleo-beaver."
—Dallas, age 7

XIII

**Maya:** I'm creative, and I like rollerblading and running. I also like Minecraft.

"Sometimes I explode with feelings. I'm a bear!"
—Maya, age 14

**River:** I like exercising and eating healthy and playing games on my tablet.

"My feelings habit animal is a beaver. I'm a perfectionist, and I think about things a lot."
—River, age 9

**Aarya:** I am a big animal person, and I like to read and write.

"Sometimes I hate myself for feeling feelings. My feelings habit animal is a deer but also a dragon since I'm a little bit of all of them."
—Aarya, age 10

**Matteo:** I like to play video games, and I also like to play soccer and baseball.

"I blow up like a bear when I get mad."
—Matteo, age 8

**Sofia:** I enjoy reading and writing, as well as spending time with my pet rabbit.

"My feelings habit animal is a chameleon. I hide my emotions from myself, but sometimes I don't have enough energy to hide them."
—Sofia, age 14

**Marcos:** I like to play sports, and I like to win.

"I push my feelings down, and sometimes I can't contain them. My mind sometimes replays bad things that happen. I am 50% chameleon and 50% beaver."
—Marcos, age 11

**Abbie:** I like being active. I like doing sports and am very happy around animals.

"Sometimes I stuff my feelings until I explode. I am mostly a bear but also a chameleon."
—Abbie, age 12

Join the Kids Team!

Color the outline how you'd like to look on this adventure. Feel free to be creative.

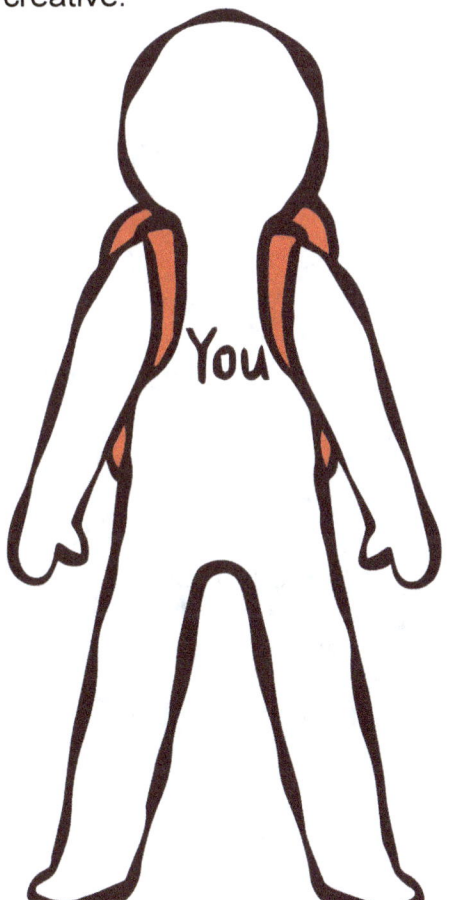

Write a quote about your feelings habit animals in the oval.

When you see this outline for "You" in our adventures, you can color it any way you wish.

XV

# Our Adventures Begin...

# Adventures in Foundation Forest!

"Our quest begins in Foundation Forest!"

"But don't tell Doodles the dolphin about our suprise party!"

What is your favorite dessert? Cookies, cake, ice cream, or something else? Becoming resilient and self-compassionate is like making a sweet treat.

First, we start with a few basic ingredients. To make a cake, we can start with flour, eggs, butter and more, which we can mix together to begin creating the batter.

In the case of self-compassion and resilience, our "batter" is made of things like noticing our emotions, being aware of our five senses, and remembering that we are not alone when hard things happen.

Later, we will add sweeteners and create a magical potion, but we'll start with the ingredients in Foundation Forest to create the batter for our magical treat!

"We will travel to six lands in Foundation Forest to collect the batter ingredients for our magical cake."

# In our first adventure, we'll visit the Land of Connection.

"Connection can make difficult feelings easier to bear."

"Did you say "bear"?! I'm a bear, and I have BIG feelings!"

"Yes! And our first comic will feature James. His feelings habit animal is a bear."

**MEET OUR FIRST COMIC CHARACTER, JAMES**

James is a big basketball fan. James gets really excited when he is looking forward to something, and he gets really mad or sad when things don't work out. James' feelings habit animal is a bear.

"Do you know what your feelings habit animal is? If not, take the quiz in the introduction to find out!"

"Join Marcos and Maya for this adventure in the Land of Connection and discover that it's human to have feelings. You'll get the first ingredient for the magical cake when you complete this adventure!"

"I'll come along 'cuz I'm your buddy!"

## IS IT OKAY TO FEEL THIS?

Did you know that there are scientists who study emotions? Scientists have studied babies, and they discovered that human babies are born with a variety of feelings including anger, fear, curiosity, joy, sadness, surprise and disgust.

As we grow, we feel many more emotions including jealousy, disappointment, shame, compassion and guilt. Guilt is a feeling that we get when we do something wrong. Shame is a feeling that we have when we are afraid that we are not a good person. Compassion is a warm feeling that we get when we greet struggles with kindness.

Do you ever tell yourself the story that if you just do everything "right" you can avoid tricky emotions? Take a look again at the feelings we are born with (anger, disgust, curiosity, sadness, fear, joy, and surprise). How many of those emotions are kind of hard to feel sometimes?

Because we are born with these feelings, they belong. Self-compassion helps us remember we are not alone when we feel hard feelings. Instead of telling ourselves that these feelings are bad, we can remind ourselves that everyone feels tricky feelings sometimes.

# A Note For What to Expect on Our Adventures

Each of our adventures will have a comic, a scroll, four activities, and "take-aways." At the end of each adventure, you can color the stars for the parts of the adventure that you completed.

Throughout our adventures, the feelings habit animals will pop in, and real kids from the Kids' Team will share their experiences.

Challenge yourself to read and do as many of the activities as you can, and ask for help if you need it. Your best is enough. **And now, on to our activities in the Land of Connection!**

# Activity 1.1 Feelings Emojis — What do You Feel?

We all feel different emotions throughout each day. Sometimes things go well and we feel really good. Other times we have difficult experiences or thoughts and we feel yucky.

What do you commonly feel? Circle the emojis that you feel a lot. You can make a few of your own and add the eyes and mouth to the blank faces.

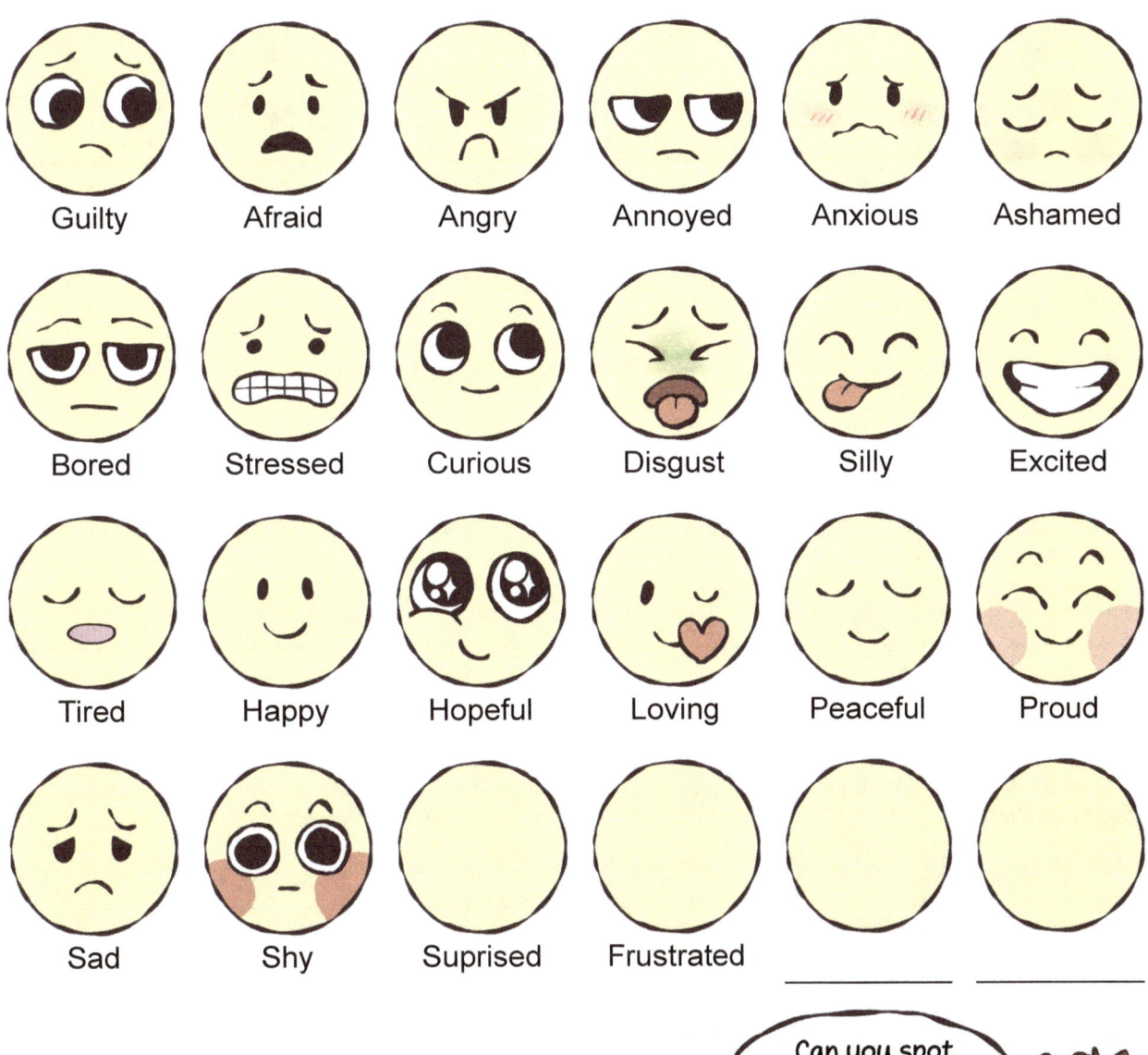

Can you spot your feelings?

**Practicing self-compassion begins with noticing how you feel.**

# Activity 1.2 When do Feelings Pop Up?

Sometimes there are situations that lead to different emotions. When do you notice different emotions popping up?

You can do this activity on your own and write your responses below, or you can do this exercise with a partner (maybe a grown-up) and speak out loud your responses.

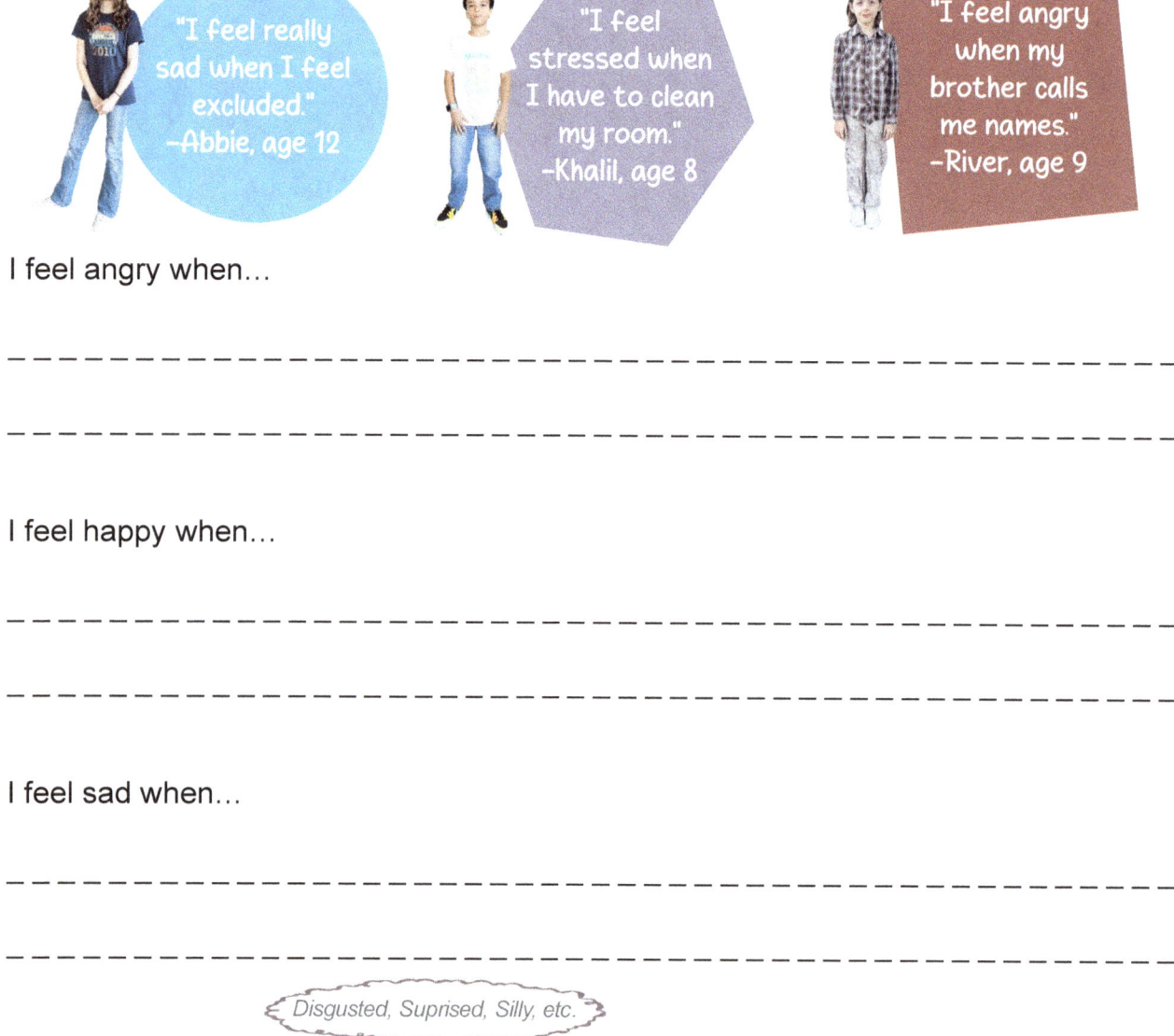

"I feel really sad when I feel excluded."
—Abbie, age 12

"I feel stressed when I have to clean my room."
—Khalil, age 8

"I feel angry when my brother calls me names."
—River, age 9

I feel angry when…

_____

_____

I feel happy when…

_____

_____

I feel sad when…

_____

_____

*Disgusted, Suprised, Silly, etc.*

I feel _____ when _____

_____

## Activity 1.3 Piano Key Feelings

Humans feel a lot of different feelings, including anger, sadness, joy, fear, curiosity, shame and many others. We have emotions to keep us safe and connected to others. For example, fear can keep us from jumping off a cliff.

In the below activity, emotions are compared to keys on a piano. Have you ever noticed that a lot of songs have both high and low notes? Imagine singing a song with only half the notes. This is what it would be like if we had only half of our feelings.

Aarya (from the Kids Team) sometimes wishes that she could get rid of sadness, fear, guilt, anger, anxiety, and shame. If she only colored the piano keys that she wanted to keep, her piano would look like this:

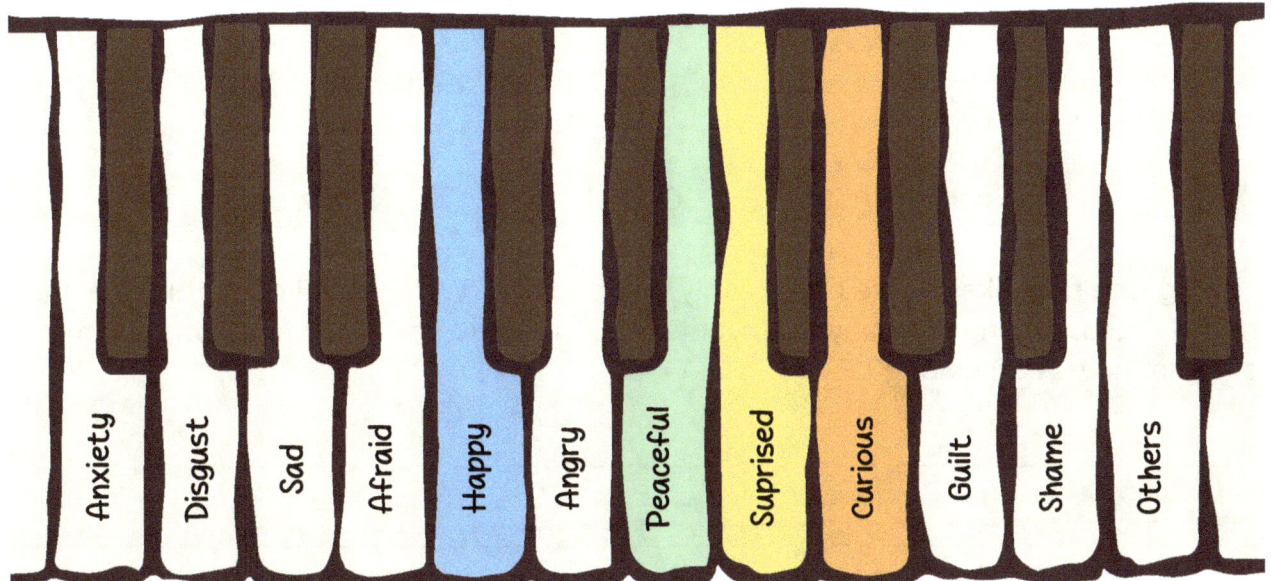

What about you? Which emotions do you sometimes wish to get rid of?

_____

_____

What feelings do I want to avoid? There's a long list. How about I tell you which one I'd like to keep. I'll take happy!

*Color the keys on this piano for the emotions that you would like to keep.*

Anxiety | Disgust | Sad | Afraid | Happy | Angry | Peaceful | Suprised | Curious | Guilt | Shame | Others

Imagine a piano with only one piano key. How could you play a song with only one note? Try to sing or hum your favorite song (or the happy birthday song) without letting your voice go up or down. How does the music sound?

Good        Okay        Not Good

Having one piano key is like having only one emotion. We need all of our emotions to be fully human. Sing or hum your favorite song. How do you feel when you hear the different notes in the song?

_____

_____

**Even if the low notes sometimes feel tricky, we need the full range of our emotions to play a beautiful song. Having emotions is part of what makes us human and connected to one another.**

*Note: People are made to feel different emotions throughout each day. If you feel like you are stuck in the same tricky feeling day after day, tell a trusted grown-up so that they can help your piano key get unstuck.*

# Activity 1.4 Human, Just Like Me

Sometimes when we have difficult emotions like fear or sadness, we feel lonely. Does this ever happen to you? It can be super helpful to remember that our feelings are okay, and other kids sometimes feel like us, too.

Even though our struggles may be different, if you imagine any person at school, at home, or in the world, you can know that they are a human being just like you. And they also sometimes have difficult feelings.

*You can do the exercise below on your own, or you can ask an adult to read it to you or help you listen to an audio recording at*
*https://jamielynntatera.com/workbook-for-kids-guided-practices/*

Begin by imagining a person who you care about - it could be someone at school, a friend, or someone in your family.
What is the name of this person? _ _ _ _ _ _ _ _ _ _ _ _ _ _ _ _ _ _ _ _ _ _

If you like, you can picture this person in your mind while you repeat or reflect on these ideas:

### Human...Just like Me*

This person is a human being, just like me.

This person has a mind and a body, just like me.

This person has feelings, thoughts and emotions, just like me.

This person has both ups and downs, just like me.

This person sometimes feels sad, angry, lonely or scared, just like me.

This person wishes hard feelings would go away, just like me.

This person wishes to be safe and happy and loved, just like me.

And anytime I feel happy or sad or lonely or scared, I can remember that this person is a fellow human being, just like me.

*This guided practice is used in the Self-Compassion for Children and Caregivers program and has been adapted from Chade-Meng Tan's "Just Like Me" practice from "Search Inside Yourself."

Take a moment to notice how you are feeling. You can draw or write about how you feel after doing this exercise or just reflect on it in your mind.

> It's great to do this anytime to help yourself remember that you are not alone, and there are others who sometimes feel like you.

"Noticing your feelings and remembering that other kids sometimes feel like you is our first resilience habit!"

# Adventure 1 Take-Aways

**Resilience Habit Animals**

 = Buddy - I'm not alone / It's okay to feel this way

 = Spots - Noticing your five senses, feelings, or thoughts

"You can circle your favorite ideas!"

### Ideas:

- It's okay (it's human!) to feel different emotions, including tricky ones.
- There are other kids, just like you, who sometimes feel like you.

### Helpful Practices:

- Notice your feelings throughout the day.
- Human, Just Like Me: You can listen to the guided audio to remind yourself that you're not alone.

### Bonus Activity:

Piano Key Feelings: You could make an art project with piano key feelings and color all the notes. Then hang it somewhere to remember that all emotions belong.

### Curiosity Question:

Who do you know who sometimes feels emotions like you?

**A Note for Grown-Ups:**
When you see a child struggling with difficult emotions, you can remind them that it's okay to feel how they feel. If a child is open to the idea, you can help them remember that there are other kids who sometimes feel like they feel. You can also do this for yourself when you are struggling. Caring for children can sometimes be tiring. You are not alone!

# Bear is having a hard moment. Let's help Bear use Buddy's helpful habit.

# In our next adventure, we'll visit the Land of Freedom

"This land will help us feel free to feel all our feelings!"

"Really? Is that possible? That would be so nice."

**MEET OUR SECOND COMIC CHARACTER, ANITA**

Anita is a kind friend. She sometimes worries that it's wrong to feel mad or sad. Anita likes to play piano but fears she is not good enough. Her feelings habit animals are a deer and a beaver.

"Do you know what your feelings habit animal is? Wait, I already asked that. Sometimes I think the same thought over and over and over…"

Join River and Anjali for an adventure in the Land of Freedom. You'll discover that it's okay to feel all your feelings and get the next ingredient for the magical cake!

## *CAN I HAVE MULTIPLE FEELINGS?*

Sometimes, like Anita, we might tell ourselves that we should feel one way and not another. Feelings are not right or wrong—they are just feelings! How we respond to our feelings is what is important. When we feel difficult emotions, we want to remind ourselves that it is natural. We don't have to act on all of our emotions or believe all our thoughts, but we do want to let ourselves feel our feelings. Challenging emotions will pass on their own if we greet them with kindness.

In addition to creating space for tricky emotions, we also want to create space for positive emotions like gratefulness, compassion, curiosity and happiness. In the comic, Curi encouraged Anita to get curious about whether she could be a little jealous and also a little happy for her friend. We don't have to choose between this or that emotion. What is it like for you to let yourself have BOTH tricky emotions and positive ones at the same time?

Sometimes one feeling will be big and another feeling will be so small it's hard to notice. We want to welcome and accept all our feelings—even seemingly different feelings at the same time.

I wonder how many feelings a person can feel at the same time?

## Activity 2.1 Side-by-Side Feelings

Sometimes in life we have more than one emotion side-by-side. For example, before performing, you might feel a little nervous and also a little excited (nervouscited).

Maya (from the Kids Team) connected feelings that she has felt at the same time. When Maya's sister took her stickers, she felt mad and also sad, so she connected mad and sad, and then created a new word - smad.

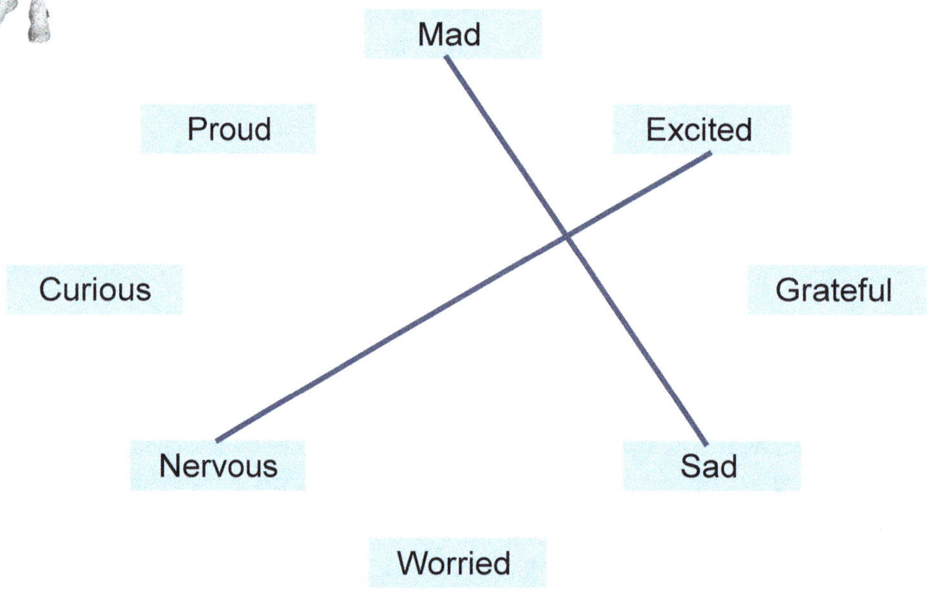

Mad

Proud          Excited

Curious          Grateful

Nervous          Sad

Worried

____Mad____ + ____Sad____ = ____Smad____

____Nervous____ + ____Excited____ = ____Nervouscited____

"I feel upset+sad+annoyed (upsenoyed) when people don't listen to me." –Matteo, age 8

What feelings have you had at the same time? Draw a line to connect your side-by-side feelings, and then make a new word by mixing them together. Feel free to add extra feelings. Be creative and use your imagination!

*Joy + Hopeful = Hoy. Khalil, age 8*

Mad

_____

Nervous          Proud

Curious          Disgust

Excited          Grateful

Happy            Bored

Sad              Tired

Shame            Joy

Worried          Hopeful

_____ + _____ = _____

_____ + _____ = _____

_____ + _____ = _____

If you'd like, try 3 feelings!

_____ + _____ + _____ = _____

# Activity 2.2 Big and Little Feelings

Sometimes when we have side-by-side feelings, one feeling is big and another feeling is small.

Here are some examples from the Kids Team:

When people ignore Sofia's feelings, she feels very sad and a little angry. Her feelings look like this:

When Dallas's brother got a prize, he felt very jealous and a little happy. His feelings looked like this:

When Khalil tried out for baseball, he felt very, very nervous and a little excited. In Khalil's example, his feelings looked like this:

When have you felt a mix of big and little feelings? Write about a time when you had one big feeling and one little feeling. Then draw a picture to show the size of your big and little feelings.

_____

_____

_____

_____

# Activity 2.3 Feeling Foods

Imagine that your emotions are like food. Enjoyable feelings could be foods that you really like, and challenging feelings could be foods that you don't like. Happiness could be your favorite fruit, ice cream, or some other yummy food. Shame might be liver, onions, or some other food that you don't enjoy.

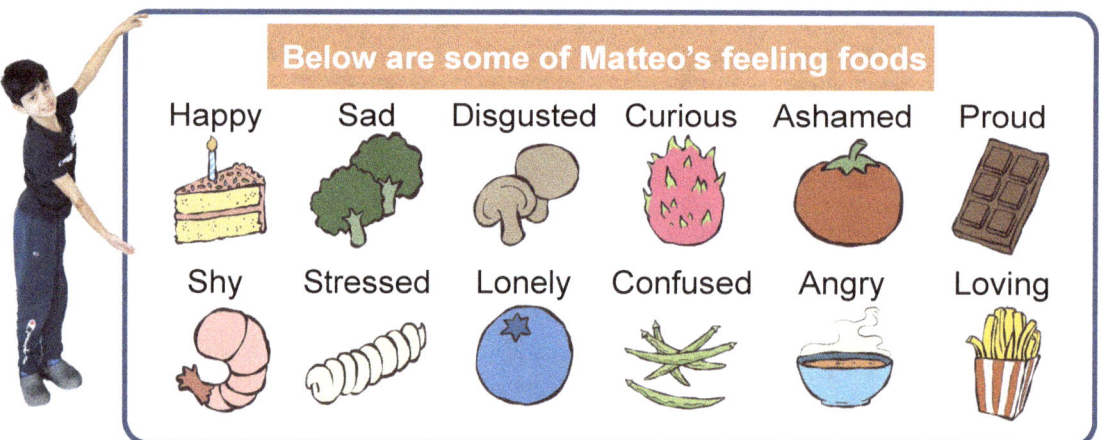

Now it's your turn! You can use these and other food ideas for the feelings below. Do the emotions you think are most important and/or fill in the blanks for extra emotions not written.

| Happy | Sad | Scared | Ashamed |
|---|---|---|---|
|  |  |  |  |
| Grateful | _____ | _____ | _____ |

# Activity 2.4 Share the Plate

If you imagine having a plate, at different times during the day, you will have different foods (emotions) on your plate. Sometimes you will have many emotions on your plate at the same time.

> When Abbie (from the Kids Team) started a new school, she felt sad, stressed, hopeful, curious, shy, and excited.

If you imagine Abbie's emotions being foods on a plate, her new school plate would look like this:

Sometimes kids ignore or push foods off their plate. If Abbie pushed away difficult emotions, her feelings plate would look like this:

You can color the foods that were pushed off the plate. These feelings count, too.

Do you ever push difficult emotions off your plate? _ _ _ _ _ _ _ _ _ _ _ _

Other times, kids get stuck in hard feelings and forget about positive feelings. If Abbie only focused on difficult emotions, her feelings plate would look like this:

Do you sometimes forget to make space for positive emotions? _ _ _ _ _ _ _ _
Positive emotions include compassion as well as gratitude, happiness, and more!

Think of a time when you tried something new or different. Did you have more than one feeling? You can look at the feeling foods in the last activity for ideas.

_____

_____

Draw the foods or write the feelings you had when you tried something new.

Do you think you could make space for all of your emotions—the ones that feel good and the ones that feel tricky—on one plate?

How did you feel when you were given this activity book? Was there a mix of emotions? If you want to draw or write about it, you can use the box below.

> To be happier over time, we want to accept difficult feelings and grow positive feelings, too.

**A Note for Grown-Ups:**
Some kids need help noticing positive emotions. The timing of this is important. We can help kids spot positive feelings when they are not upset.

# Adventure 2 Take-Aways

**Resilience Habit Animals**

 = Buddy - I'm not alone / It's okay to feel this way

 = Spots - Noticing your five senses, feelings, or thoughts

 = Sunny - Thinking of good things

*You can circle your favorite ideas!*

### Ideas:

 You can have more than one emotion at the same time (side-by-side feelings).

 It is helpful to share the plate with different emotions.

### Helpful Practices:

 Notice and name side-by-side feelings.

 When you are stuck in one emotion, get curious about sharing the plate with other feelings (including self-compassion and love).

### Bonus Activity:

Pick a situation, and get curious about all the different emotions that a person could feel in that situation.

### Curiosity Question:

How many different emotions can you feel at the same time?

---

**A Note for Grown-Ups:**
What is something that you have side-by-side feelings about? Appropriately sharing with kids your own "side-by-side" feelings is a great way to help kids know that it's okay to feel a variety of feelings.

Sometimes kids feel strong negative emotions and grown-ups can be tempted to push children's negative emotions off their plates. It's important that we allow kids to fully feel difficult emotions (and give yourself kindness because it can be hard to witness).

# Deer is struggling. Let's help Deer use Spots' & Buddy's helpful habits.

# In our next adventure, we'll visit the Land of Mindfulness.

"Spots, what's mindfulness?"

"Oh! I love mindfulness! It's noticing what's happening in the moment. Like right now I'm noticing that my neck feels cold."

**MEET OUR THIRD COMIC CHARACTER, SAM**

Sam likes to look at things logically and also loves building with legos. Sam's feelings habit animal is a chameleon.

"I think Sam also has the beaver habit 'cuz Sam's thinking can be a little sticky..."

*Join Sofia and Matteo for an adventure in the Land of Mindfulness. You'll strengthen your ability to notice the now and get the next ingredient for the magical cake!*

*Mindfulness is my favorite. I'm coming too!*

## WHAT IS MINDFULNESS?

Take a moment and notice how you feel while reading this book. Do you feel curious? Frustrated? Bored? Peaceful? When you notice how you feel, you are practicing mindfulness. Now notice the position of your body. Can you feel your hands touching the book or your feet touching the floor? Noticing how your body feels is mindfulness, too. You can also notice the color of this note or the smell of the book (does it have a smell?). When you get curious about your five senses, you are practicing mindfulness!

Mindfulness is noticing what is happening in this moment. Just like any skill, we can strengthen our mindfulness power with practice. Curiosity can make it easier to be mindful. When we are curious about our five senses, it can be easier to pay attention to what's going on around us. When we are curious about our thoughts and feelings, it can help us notice what's happening inside of us.

Mindfulness is like a friend that can help you focus your attention in the moment at any time. If you'd like to grow your resilience superpower, try to be curious about what is happening in your mind, body, and the world around you.

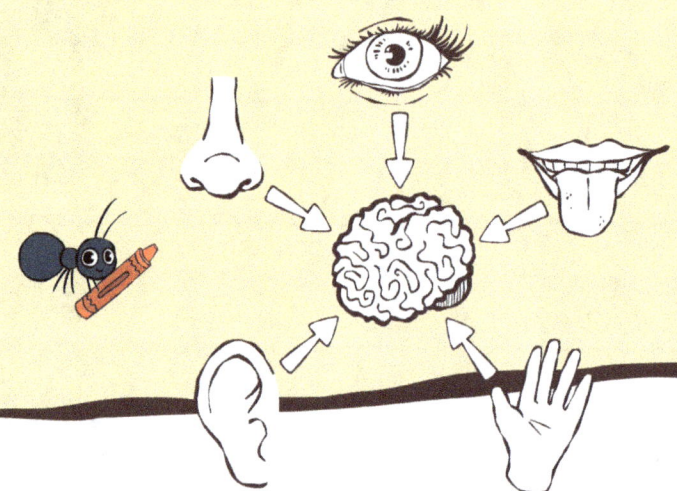

## Activity 3.1 Curiosity is a Superpower

This activity explores the power of curiosity and how curiosity can help us to be mindful. We can get curious about our emotions, thoughts, five senses, and how our body feels.

Did you notice that there is an ant in every comic? Does your brain get curious about where to find the ant? You can try this out with the picture below. There are 10 ants in the picture.

**How many ants can you find?** _____

*Coloring can be a way to practice mindfulness.*

How hard was it to <u>focus</u> on the picture to find the ant? Circle your response.

Easy to focus        In between        Hard to focus

**Mindfulness becomes more fun when we get curious about what we can see, hear, smell, taste, and feel. Instead of paying attention, it feels more like "playing attention."**

## Activity 3.2 Feel Your Feet

You can "play attention" to the soles of your feet. You can be curious about the sensations in your feet and toes, such as warm, cool, tingly, ticklish, or neutral (nothing).

Move your foot.* Now try wiggling your toes. Which toes can you feel? Your little toe, your big toe, your middle toes? Which toe is easier to move?

_____

_____

Can you feel your toes and the bottoms of your feet when you are still? What can you feel?

_____

_____

> I can feel my middle feet easier!

Try moving around. You can stand up and notice the pressure on your feet.* Take a stroll around or jump up and down. Now stop and notice how your feet feel.

_____

_____

*Note: If you are not able to move your feet, you can do this exercise with your hands.

Now try tracing your foot or toes (this can be fun to do with a partner). Notice what you can feel. Note: If you don't feel comfortable placing your foot on this book, you could trace your toes with your finger.

Place your foot in this box, and then trace the outline of your foot or toes with a pencil. After you are done, circle the toes that you feel most easily.

Is it easier to feel your foot and toes after you trace it?

☐ Yes
☐ No

> **If you practice feeling your feet over time, it will become easier to notice how they feel. Focusing on the sensations of your feet can help bring you into the moment. You can notice any part of your body in this way.**

# Activity 3.3 Mindful Seeing and Listening

Mindfulness can help us to notice what is happening right now. Let's get curious about what we can see and hear.

👀 Look around the room. What do you see (colors, textures, shapes)?

Is there anything that you haven't noticed before? A small crack or speck of paint?

_____

_____

*Do you see anything that you enjoy looking at? Draw a picture or write about that object.*

Now turn your attention to listening 👂. Close your eyes if that feels comfortable. What can you hear? Can you hear sounds inside the room? Outside the room? Inside your body (breathing, etc.)?

_____

_____

Now, let's check and see which you enjoy more—seeing or listening.

  Look around the room, and notice how you feel.

  Now, close your eyes and listen to sounds, and notice how you feel.

Which did you prefer?

☐ Seeing
☐ Listening

Why did you prefer that?

_____

_____

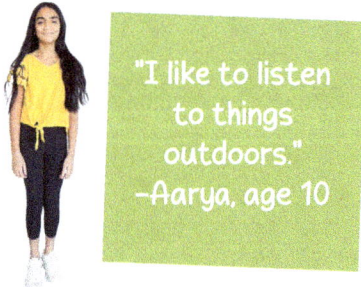

"I like to listen to things outdoors."
—Aarya, age 10

"I like seeing because it is colorful."
—Khalil, age 8

**Mindfully listening and seeing can help you notice what is happening in the moment, and you can practice this at any time.**

# Activity 3.4 Puppy Dog Mind Training

We can be mindful of our thinking. Pause for a minute and notice your thoughts. After you are done, write your thoughts in the thought bubble.

Our minds can get distracted just like puppies can. Puppies and minds are alike. If we want a puppy to sit, we have to train it. And if we want our minds to notice the present moment, we will have to train our puppy mind.

To train a puppy, we give it a treat every time it does the right thing—again and again and again.

If we are trying to train our puppy mind to notice the now, everytime we come back to the present moment, we can give ourselves a mental 'thumbs up!' (like a treat).

Our puppy mind training goes like this:

Step 1 = Distracted Mind

Step 2 = Come back to the moment

Step 3 = Treat (Mental Thumbs up)

**Follow the pattern to help the puppy get the bone.**

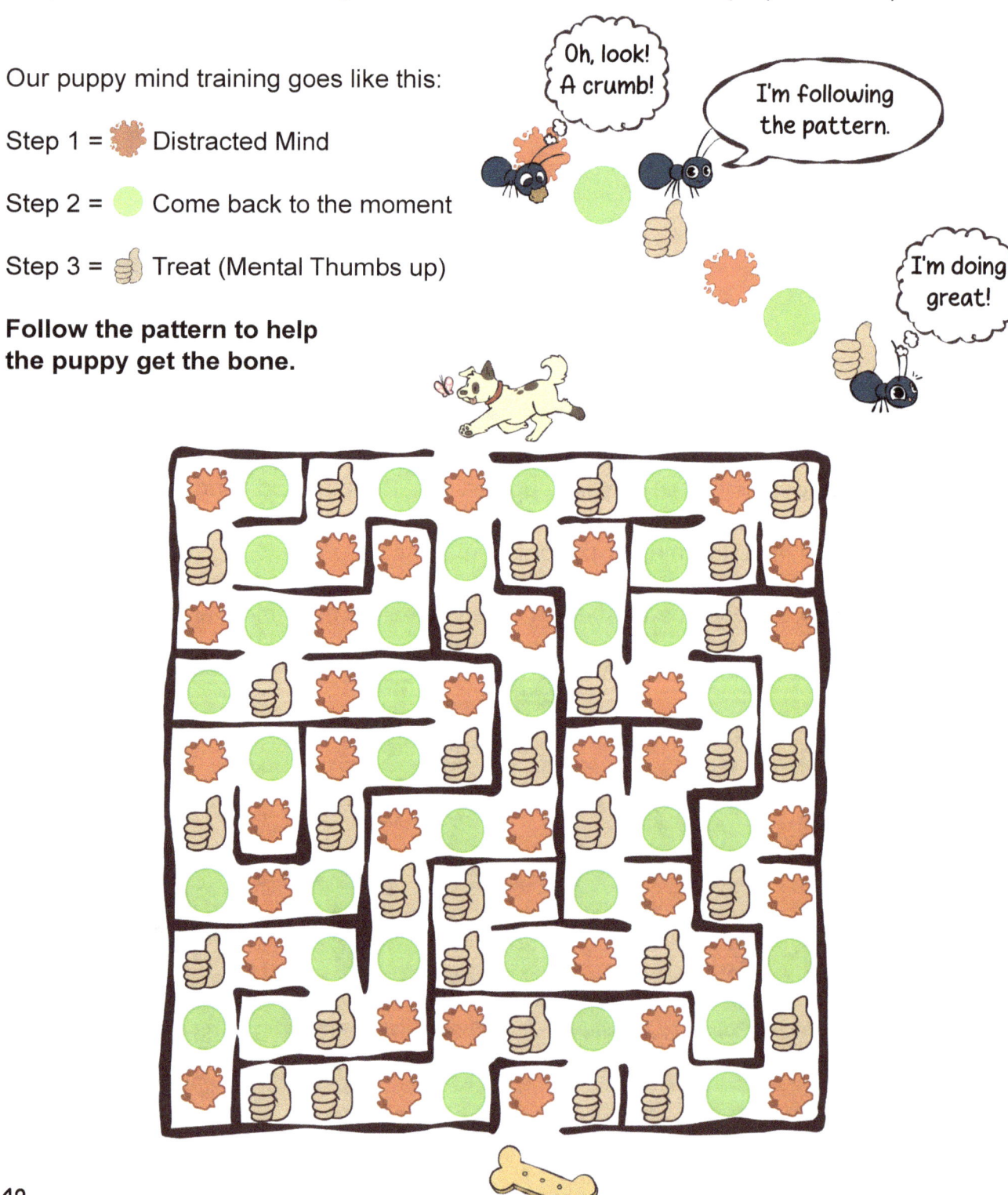

Pick one of these sensory experience to focus on:

- [ ] Seeing (see page 39)
- [ ] Listening (see page 39)
- [ ] Feeling Your Feet (see pages 36-37)

Try focusing your attention on seeing, listening, or feeling your feet for **one minute**. Your brain will definitely start thinking about other things.

To train your puppy mind, notice when your mind is distracted, and then again notice the sense that you have chosen (seeing, listening, or feeling your feet). Remember to treat yourself to a mental thumbs up after you come back to noticing the now. Repeat the pattern. Starting now.

How did your puppy mind respond to the training?

_____

_____

"When I get distracted, it's hard to get back in the moment." –River, age 9

"I noticed that being curious helps me to focus on the now." –Maya, age 14

"I realized I beat myself up when my mind wanders too much." –Aarya, age 10

Remember, your mind will not stay put. We are practicing helping our mind come back to the present. It takes A LOT of practice (and mental thumbs up) to train a puppy mind, but you will have more happiness and freedom when your puppy mind learns to come when it's called…even just for a moment!

# Adventure 3 Take-Aways

**Resilience Habit Animal**

 = Spots - Noticing your five senses, feelings, or thoughts

*You can circle your favorite ideas!*

### Ideas:

 Practicing mindfulness can help us be in the moment.

 Curiosity can make it feel like we are "playing" attention (rather than trying to pay attention). There's a pattern to training our puppy mind: distracted mind, notice the now, mental 'thumbs up'…repeat.

### Helpful Practices:

 Get curious about how your body feels, including your feet and toes.

 Practice mindful seeing and listening.

 Practice puppy mind training.

### Bonus Activity:

Play "I Spy" by yourself or with a partner.

- If you are playing with a partner, you and your partner can take turns choosing the color of an object and saying, "I spy with my little eye something <u>(the color of the object)</u>." The other person will guess which object you have chosen.

- If you are playing on your own, pick a color before you look around. Then ask yourself, "Can I spy with my little eye something <u>(the color you have chosen)</u>?" Then look around and try to find an object that is the color that you have chosen.

### Curiosity Question:

What parts of your body are you not yet able to feel (in your mind)?

---

**A Note for Grown-Ups:**

**Practicing mindfulness can be challenging for kids (and grown-ups)! The more you can make practicing into a game (like playing "I Spy with my Little Eye" or "I Hear with my Little Ear"), the more kids will enjoy using their five senses on purpose. Bedtime can also be a great time to invite kids to practice a little mindfulness.**

*Join Dallas and Abbie for an adventure in the Land of Acceptance. Discover how acceptance can make down moments more manageable and get the next ingredient for the magical cake!*

*Can I get a hat this time for coming along? I love hats!!*

## WE CAN'T HAVE UPS WITHOUT DOWNS

In the comic, James got upset because part of the bike ride was hard. Sometimes we might wish to have all fun moments with no difficult moments. Unfortunately, as Curi reminded James, we can't have ups without downs.

In this activity book, we will be calling "up moments" the times that we enjoy. Can you think of an up moment?

We call the challenging moments "down moments." Down moments are those times when you feel disappointed, angry, lonely, sad, scared or stressed. Can you think of a down moment?

Sometimes our thoughts or actions might be a part of a down moment—like forgetting our homework or saying the wrong thing to a friend. When this happens, we can try to make it better. We can also remind ourselves that no one is perfect. Being hard on ourselves when we make a mistake will only make things worse.

We can remind ourselves that **imperfection and down moments are a part of life**. We can also give ourselves kindness because down moments can be really hard.

*Dropping a treat on the ground is a down moment.*

## Activity 4.1 Rollercoaster of Life

Life is full of ups, downs, and "loop-de-loops." Draw or write about some of your up moments (happy and/or excited moments) and down moments (sad and/or stressful moments) below.

"If a down moment didn't happen, then maybe an up moment wouldn't happen either."
—Abbie, age 12

"I had a down moment when I forgot my homework."
—Aarya, age 10

"When I get what I want it's an up moment, and when I don't get what I want it's a down moment."
—River, age 9

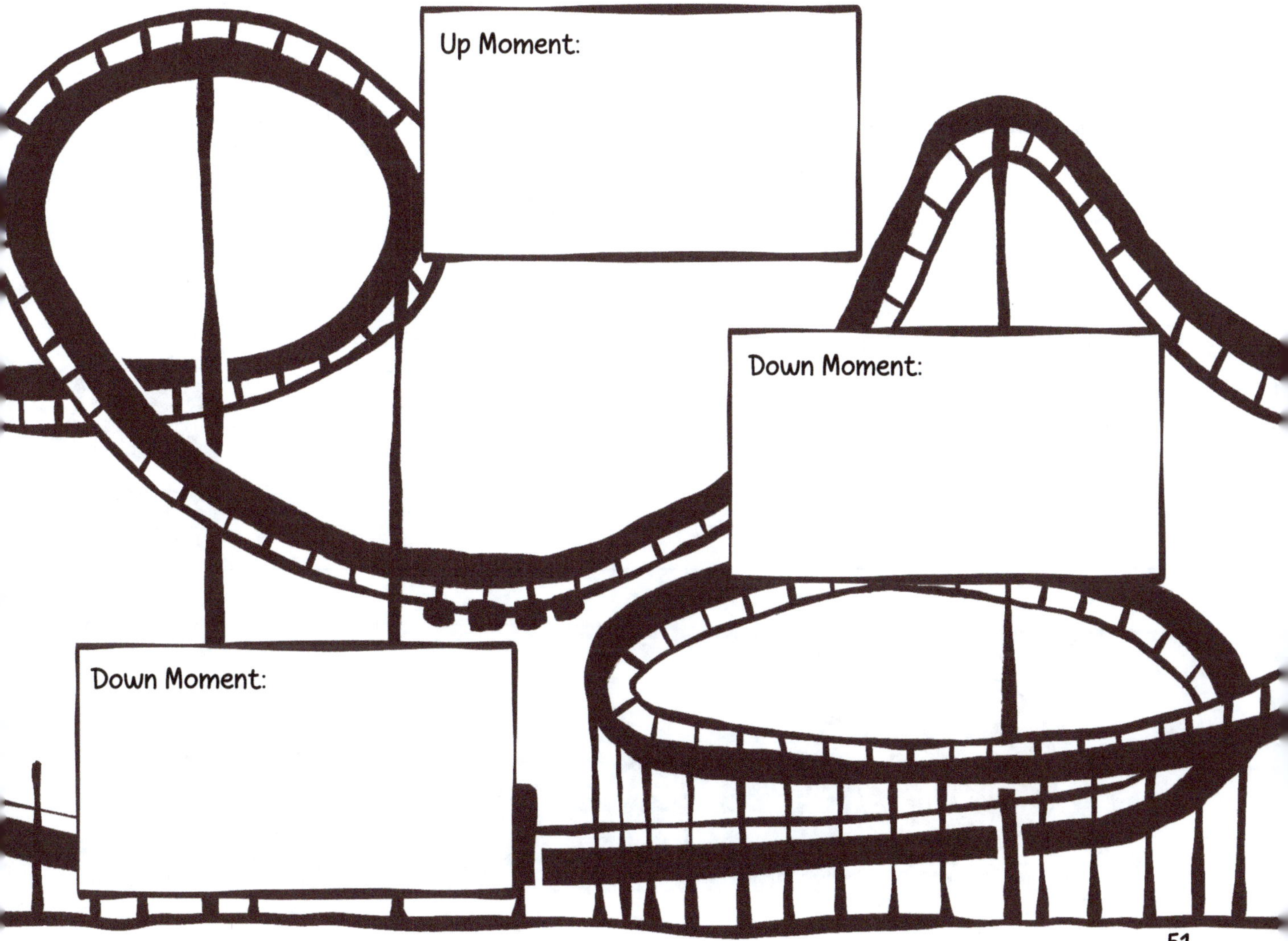

Up Moment:

Down Moment:

Down Moment:

51

## Activity 4.2 Mixed Moments

Sometimes a situation is a little up and a little down at the same time. Some moments can be bittersweet—a little bit sour and a little bit sweet. Can you think of some mixed or "side-by-side" moments?

Examples of mixed moments:

"Recess is kind of good and kind of bad because some people are nice to me and some people are not."
—Dallas, age 7

"When I lost my clarinet, I felt really sad, but then I got a new clarinet that was even better than my old one."
—Maya, age 14

Up Moment + Down Moment = Mixed Moment

MIXED MOMENTS!!?? I usually think things are all good or all bad!

Write about one of your mixed moments.

_____

_____

_____

In mixed situations, we can encourage ourselves to enjoy the up parts, and give ourselves compassion for the down parts.

# Activity 4.3 Mind Muddles

Have you ever seen your reflection in a pond or a funny-shaped mirror that makes you look a little strange? Sometimes our thinking can make reality look messed up. This kind of mixed up thinking can be called a mind muddle. Sometimes kids (and grown-ups) have mind muddles that make difficult moments even harder.

**Below are some common mind muddles. Notice which ones you sometimes have:**

**All-or-Nothing:** Seeing situations and people as being all one way or all another way, like all good or all bad.

**Should-or-Shouldn't:** Telling yourself that things should or should not be as they are.

Which mind muddle do you think kids have more often, All-or-Nothing or Should-and-Shouldn't?

- - - - - - - - - - - - - - - - - - - - - - - - - - - - - - - -

**Only-Noticing-What's-Wrong:** Focusing only on the negative and ignoring the positive.

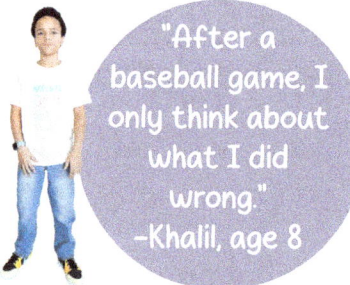

"After a baseball game, I only think about what I did wrong."
–Khalil, age 8

**Imagining-the-Worst:** Imagining bad things happening in the future.

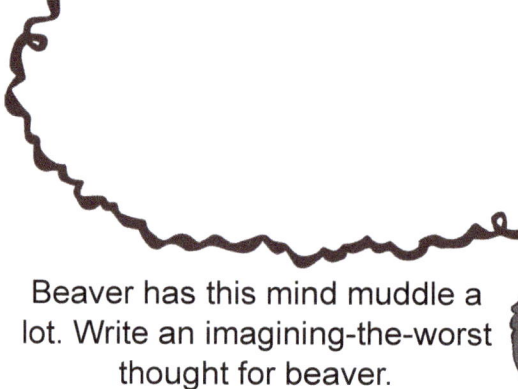

Beaver has this mind muddle a lot. Write an imagining-the-worst thought for beaver.

**All-About-Me:** We think that everything that happens is about us.

He must be upset because of me!

Remember, everyone has mind muddles sometimes.

## Activity 4.4 Mind Muddle Messages

When we notice a mind muddle, we can try to help ourselves see things more clearly.

"When I think something is 'all-about-me,' I try to remind myself not to take it personally."
—Maya, age 14

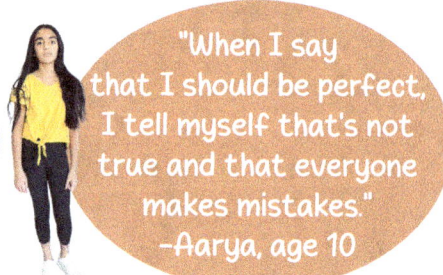

"When I say that I should be perfect, I tell myself that's not true and that everyone makes mistakes."
—Aarya, age 10

**A Helpful Message**
What do you like to say to yourself when you are having a hard time? Having a message or phrase that is just right for you can be helpful.

Here are some examples. Check the ones you like.

- ☐ Everyone makes mistakes.
- ☐ Don't take it personally.
- ☐ It's going to be okay.
- ☐ I can do hard things.
- ☐ Breathe.
- ☐ Other _ _ _ _ _ _ _ _ _ _ _ _

Make a poster for your favorite message (you can choose one from above):

Maya made her message into a poster.

Try saying your favorite message next time you are having a down moment.

The resilience habit animals have ideas for other ways you can respond to mind muddles and difficult moments.

You can try these ideas next time you are struggling. They won't make difficult feelings magically go away, but they can definitely help!

# Adventure 4 Take-Aways

### Resilience Habit Animals

 = Buddy - I'm not alone / It's okay to feel this way

 = Spots - Noticing your five senses, feelings, or thoughts

 = Sunny - Thinking of good things

 = Snuggles - Comforting or encouraging words or touch

 = Doodles - Actions that are kind to your body, mind or heart

*You can circle your favorite ideas!*

### Ideas:

 Ups and downs are a part of being human.

 Our thoughts and actions can make difficult moments easier to deal with or harder.

### Helpful Practices:

 Notice when you have a mind muddle (everyone sometimes has mind muddles!).

 Practice Buddy's, Spots', Doodles', Snuggles', or Sunny's habits to help yourself when things go wrong.

### Bonus Activity:

Think back to some difficult moments in your life. Are there any down moments that have led to up moments?

### Curiosity Question:

Can you think of a situation that can be either an up moment or a down moment (or a mixed moment) depending on how you think about it?

---

**A Note for Grown-Ups:**
Be sure to normalize resistance of down moments. While it's true that they are a part of living, sometimes kids and grown-ups need to vent because down moments can be frustrating!

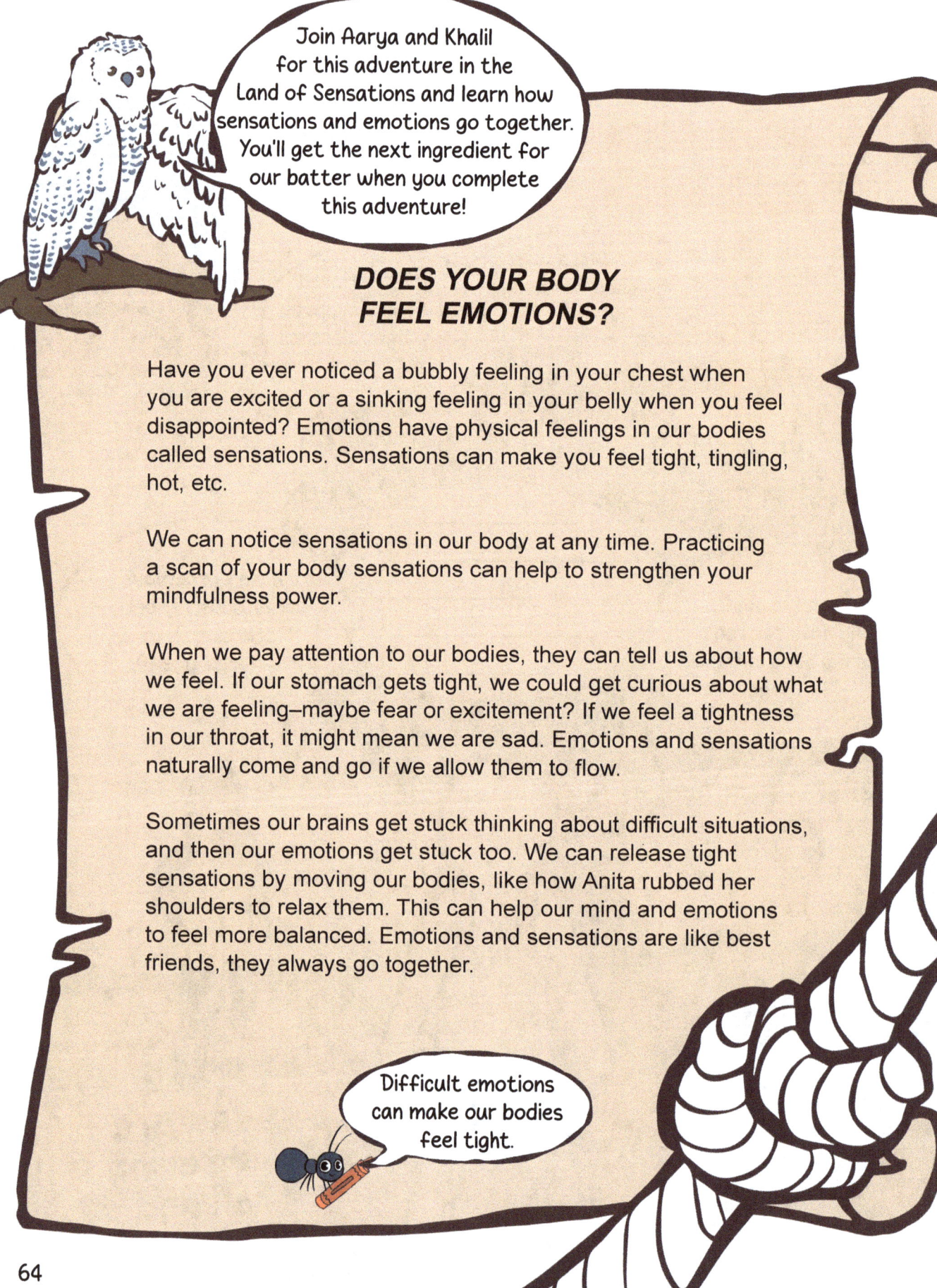

## *DOES YOUR BODY FEEL EMOTIONS?*

Have you ever noticed a bubbly feeling in your chest when you are excited or a sinking feeling in your belly when you feel disappointed? Emotions have physical feelings in our bodies called sensations. Sensations can make you feel tight, tingling, hot, etc.

We can notice sensations in our body at any time. Practicing a scan of your body sensations can help to strengthen your mindfulness power.

When we pay attention to our bodies, they can tell us about how we feel. If our stomach gets tight, we could get curious about what we are feeling—maybe fear or excitement? If we feel a tightness in our throat, it might mean we are sad. Emotions and sensations naturally come and go if we allow them to flow.

Sometimes our brains get stuck thinking about difficult situations, and then our emotions get stuck too. We can release tight sensations by moving our bodies, like how Anita rubbed her shoulders to relax them. This can help our mind and emotions to feel more balanced. Emotions and sensations are like best friends, they always go together.

> Join Aarya and Khalil for this adventure in the Land of Sensations and learn how sensations and emotions go together. You'll get the next ingredient for our batter when you complete this adventure!

> Difficult emotions can make our bodies feel tight.

# Activity 5.1 X-Ray Yourself

*Look at the sensations below and check off the ones that you feel.*

**Sensations** are physical feelings in the body.

- ☐ Light
- ☐ Sweaty
- ☐ Heavy
- ☐ Empty
- ☐ Tight
- ☐ Tingling
- ☐ Cold
- ☐ Warm
- ☐ Numb
- ☐ Droopy
- ☐ Itchy
- ☐ Relaxed
- ☐ _____
- ☐ _____

Imagine you had a special x-ray that could see your sensations. If you could x-ray your body for sensations, what would they look like?

Marcos, from the Kids Team, felt these sorts of sensations in his body. He drew his emotions in the outline below, and then he created a key to show his different sensations.

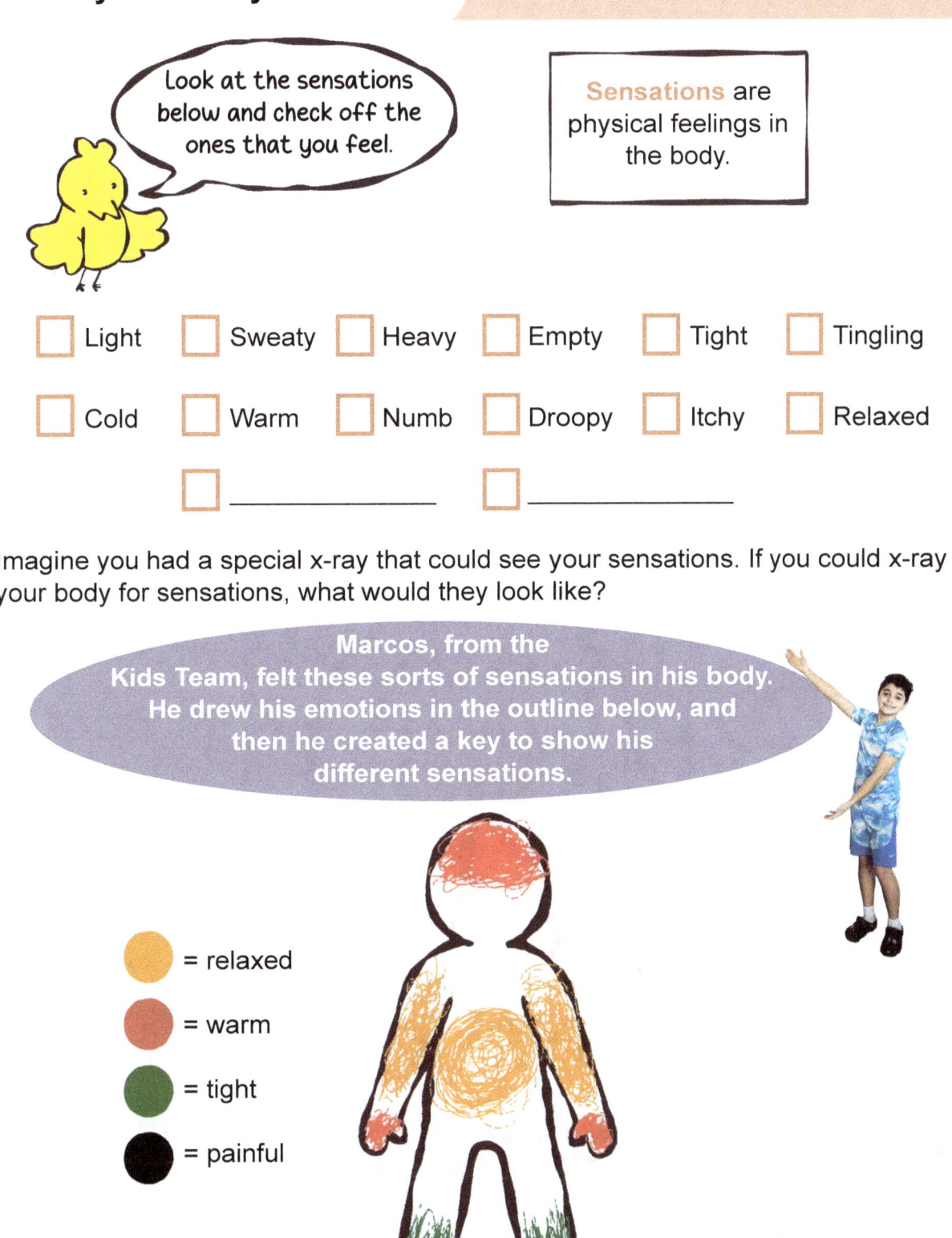

● = relaxed
● = warm
● = tight
● = painful

Imagine that you are x-raying your body sensations now. Notice your foot. What does it feel like? Is it warm, cold, tingly, prickly, numb, sweaty? Move up your body and notice what you feel. **Draw colors or symbols to show how your body feels.** X-ray your body part by part noticing sensations.

**Draw colors for the sensations in your body:**

**Noticing sensations in your body can center your mind.**

*A Note for Grown-Ups:*

*A body scan ("x-ray") is a great activity for children (and grown-ups) to do after exercising or before bed.*

# Activity 5.2 Color Your Feelings

Have you ever felt your stomach or shoulders tighten when you got angry? Emotions have physical sensations (feelings) in the body. Every emotion has different sensations.

**Maya's examples:**
When I feel excited, I get a light feeling in my shoulders. It feels sparkly yellow. When I feel disappointed, I feel a sinking feeling in my belly, like a black, deflated balloon.

Excited      Disappointed

 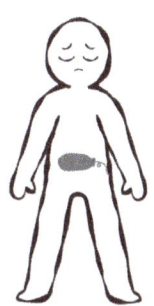

Pretend like you are feeling the emotions below, and notice where you feel the sensations in your body. Choose a color to represent each feeling and color the parts of the body where you have sensations.

Angry      Happy      Afraid

 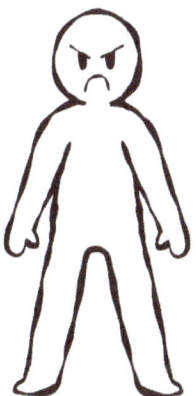  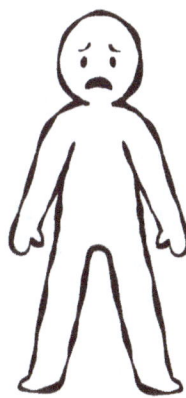

"My face gets hot when I feel mad."
—Dallas, age 7

"I felt happiness in my heart, and I chose green."
—Khalil, age 8

Sad         Embarrassed         Peaceful

Feel free to write about any body sensations that you feel when you have different emotions.

_____

_____

_____

 "Sometimes I feel mad and sad at the same time, and my body feels kind of tight and kind of loose."
—River, age 9

 "My chest feels tight when I am stressed and also when I'm excited. But when I'm excited it feels tight in a good way."
—Abbie, age 12

Emotion has the word motion inside of it, and emotions have to move through our bodies! Noticing sensations when we have tricky emotions can help them to move through us (instead of getting trapped inside!).

# Activity 5.3 Squeeze and Soften

When we have difficult emotions, sometimes parts of our bodies get tight. What emotions make your body feel tight?

_____

_____

It can be helpful to relax tight parts of our body. One way to do this is tightening parts of our body on purpose and then releasing the tension. If you like, you can hold your breath for a moment while tightening, and then open your mouth and breathe out, "Ahhhh…" while you soften.

 Let's try this now. You can do this exercise on your own, or you can ask an adult to read it to you or help you listen to an audio recording:
https://jamielynntatera.com/workbook-for-kids-guided-practices/

### Squeeze and Soften

Get in a comfortable position to do this exercise (seated or lying down).

Start by squeezing the muscles in your feet. Hoooooooolllllllllldddddddd…. Then release and soften.

Now tighten the muscles in your legs and bottom. Breathe in and hoooooooolllllllllldddddddd…. Then release and breathe out your mouth with a sigh, ahhhh…

Next, squeeze the muscles of your stomach and back. Hooooooolllllllllldddddddd… Then release and soften.

Tense the muscles in your arms and hands. Breathe in and hoooooooolllllllllldddddddd…. Then release and breathe out your mouth with a sigh, ahhhh…

Now, squeeze the muscles of your shoulders and chest. Hoooooolllllllllldddddd…. Then release and soften.

Finally, tighten the muscles in your face. Breathe in and hooooooolllllllllldddddddd…. Then release and breathe out your mouth with a sigh, ahhhh…

Notice how your body feels now.

This is something that you can DO when you feel stressed!

Ahhhhh…….

You can squeeze and soften body parts that get tight when you have challenging emotions.

**A Note for Grown-Ups:**

*If a child seems receptive, you can ask them where they feel emotions in their body and invite them to give any stressed body parts a little rub or a squeeze and soften.*

# Activity 5.4 Stretch Like an Animal

Stretching can help to release tight sensations from the body. Stretching can also calm our mind and emotions, especially when we take deep breaths.

Different types of animal stretches will affect your body and mind differently. You can try a variety of stretches, including strong, balancing, stretchy, and relaxed animals.

**Strong Animals**

Shark

Panther Plank

*Every body is different. Adjust the stretches for your body.*

**Balancing Animals**

Eagle

Flamingo

**Stretchy Animals**

Cat-Cow

Twisty Dolphin

Downward Dog

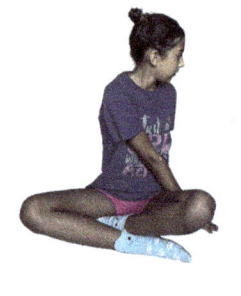

> You can take deep breaths while you do these poses.

**Relaxed Animals**

Bunny Pose

Alligator Breathing

Sloth Belly Breathing

To practice these animal stretches, you can do the maze below. Do the stretches of the animals that you encounter on the way to the sloth at the end of the maze.

Which animal stretches did you do?

_____

_____

# Adventure 5 Take-Aways

*Noticing sensations when you feel emotions is a resilience superpower!*

### Resilience Habit Animals

 = Spots - Noticing your five senses, feelings, or thoughts

 = Doodles - Actions that are kind to your body, mind or heart

*You can circle your favorite ideas!*

### Ideas:

 Emotions have sensations in our bodies.

 Calming our bodies can help to calm our minds.

### Helpful Practices:

 X-ray your body to notice your sensations.

 Be curious about sensations when you have emotions.

 Squeeze and Soften.

 Stretch like an Animal.

### Bonus Activity:

Embodying Emotions (on your own or with a partner)

- If you are doing this activity with a partner, take turns embodying an emotion (make your body look like you feel the emotion) and guess what emotion the other person is feeling.
- If you are doing this activity on your own, you can make a list of emotions on little slips of paper. Stand in front of the mirror, pick a slip of paper, and then embody that emotion.

### Curiosity Question:

What kind of an animal stretch can you make up?

### A Note for Grown-Ups:

Make a habit of noticing and talking about your body sensations, especially as they relate to your emotions (be sure to include both positive and tricky feelings). Tell children what you notice. Then you can invite children to share what they notice, too.

# Beaver is having a hard time focusing. Let's help Beaver use Doodles' helpful habit.

*Join Ambika and Sofia to learn how curiosity can help with hidden feelings. You will get our last foundational batter ingredient when you complete this adventure!*

*I'm coming along on this adventure. We need kindness to slowly open to emotions.*

## WHAT DO YOU DO WITH A DIFFICULT FEELING?

In the comic, Sam did not want to notice or name difficult emotions. Sam was avoiding challenging feelings. Everyone sometimes resists and avoids unpleasant things—it's human!

What are some activities that you resist doing? It could be cleaning your room, doing your homework, or doing dishes. Think about why you try to avoid doing these things. Often we resist because we don't like how these things make us feel. We avoid challenging feelings!

How does avoiding and resisting feelings work out? Usually, not very well. Difficult feelings and situations are a part of life; resisting usually only worsens things. Life feels better over time when we can open up and accept our emotions.
These four steps can help:

1. Notice resistance.

2. Name the difficult feelings.

3. Get curious about your feelings, notice body sensations and thoughts.

4. Be kind to yourself, difficult feelings are hard!

## Activity 6.1 Don't Think About the Pink Elephant!

Take a moment to notice the picture of the elephant below.

Close your eyes or look away from this page for ten seconds, and don't think about the pink elephant.

What were you thinking about when you tried not to think about the pink elephant?

_____

_____

Most kids either think about the pink elephant, or they think about something else and the pink elephant keeps popping up. Some kids even think about whether or not they are thinking wabout the pink elephant.

> I was thinking about my friend, but then she turned into an elephant!!

| Trying **not** to think about the elephant is **resisting**. | If the thought stuck around, it's **persisting**. |

**What we resist persists (sticks)!** Trying to make a thought go away can actually make it stick in your mind. This is also true for our emotions.

81

# The pink elephant can be a symbol of difficult emotions.

Bear, Deer, Chameleon and Beaver each have a different way of relating to emotional elephants. Circle the feelings habit animal(s) that match your feelings habits.

Chameleon hides emotional elephants.

Bear has BIG emotional elephants.

Deer is ashamed of emotional elephants.

Beaver obsesses about emotional elephants.

# Activity 6.2 What are Your Elephants?

When we resist something, we try to avoid it or make it go away. Kids (and grown-ups) sometimes resist situations, emotions, thoughts, and activities.

Maya (from the Kids Team) resists doing homework, cleaning her room, and washing dishes. These activities make her feel tired, bored and/or stressed. Because Maya doesn't like to feel bored, tired, and stressed, she tries to avoid activities that trigger these emotions.

What activities do you try to avoid doing? (Ideas: homework, chores, waking up, brushing teeth, waiting, taking turns, etc.)

_____

_____

How does thinking about these activities or doing these activities make you feel?

_____

_____

One reason you avoid the activities you listed is because you don't like how they make you feel. **The feelings that you listed above are feelings that you resist.**

I avoid doing things that I can't do perfectly because I worry that I'm not good enough.

You might also avoid other feelings that can be unpleasant.

*River (from the Kids Team) sometimes resists sadness, stress, anger, guilt and shame.*

These are River's emotional elephants that he sometimes resists.

Sad   Stressed   Mad   Ashamed   Guilty

Write the names of the emotions that you sometimes resist in the elephants below. You can color your emotional elephants and the words.

## What you resist sticks!

**Even though resisting feelings doesn't work out well, everyone resists feelings sometimes. Our first step is noticing our resistance. In our next activity, we will explore how we can open up to our emotional elephants over time.**

# Activity 6.3 Name it to Tame it

The second step of opening to our emotions is to name them.

Sometimes it might seem like an emotion (like anger or sadness) is a wild animal.

Naming the emotion can help the wild animal feel easier to manage.

Use this key to decode the message about emotions..

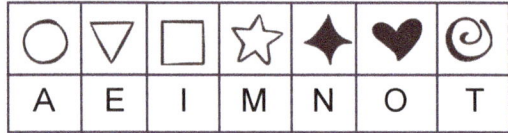

| ○ | ▽ | □ | ☆ | ◆ | ♥ | ◉ |
|---|---|---|---|---|---|---|
| A | E | I | M | N | O | T |

In the comic, Curi encouraged Sam to name feelings.
Is there someone that you feel okay talking to about your feelings?

☐ Yes
☐ No

*Talking to someone understanding can help.*

If so, who do you like to talk to? _____
If not, can you be curious about who might be a good listener?

It can be hard to talk about feelings. Luckily, there are many ways to name your emotions. Check out these ideas!

*"I write my feelings and what happened down on a piece of paper, and then I get rid of the paper."*
—Sofia, age 14

*"Sometimes I count my feelings on my fingers while I name them."*
—Khalil, age 8

*"Sometimes I just scribble if I'm angry."*
—Anjali, age 10

*"I talk to my mom and my sister about what happened. Sometimes I write it down in a secret code."*
—Maya, age 14

What is your favorite way to name emotions?

- [ ] Naming it in your mind
- [ ] Talking to someone
- [ ] Writing about it
- [ ] Telling an animal (or a stuffed animal or a tree!)
- [ ] Drawing your feelings
- [ ] Other _____

*Naming what happened can help the stories stop replaying in your mind.*

*I need that!*

Choose and circle a tricky emotion.

Practice naming the emotion you chose. If you want to draw or write about it, you can use the box below.

**Naming a difficult emotion can make it easier to bear. Name it to tame it!**

# Activity 6.4 Opening Up to Your Elephants

We've practiced the first two steps of opening to emotional elephants. We have two steps to go!

Step 1: Notice hidden elephants

Step 2: Name emotional elephants.

Step 3: Explore Emotional Elephants

Step 4: Be kind to your elephants (and yourself).

**Step 3: Explore Emotional Elephants**
Get curious about body sensations and thoughts.

In this comic, Sam was left out.

Let's practice exploring and being kind to our emotional elephants!

It might feel good to hide difficult emotions, but we'll feel better over time if we can learn to open up to our emotional elephants.

What thoughts and feelings do you think Sam might have had about being left out? What would you think and feel if it happened to you?

**Step 4: Be kind to your emotional elephants (and yourself!)**
Difficult feelings are hard. When we have hard feelings, we can wrap our elephants and ourselves in a blanket of kindness!

We can be kind to ourselves when things go wrong!

Circle the words on the blanket that can comfort the emotional elephant.

It's okay
I understand
Would you like a hug?
How can I help?
That's hard
I care about you
I love you

# Adventure 6 Take-Aways

**Resilience Habit Animals**

 = Spots - Noticing your five senses, feelings, or thoughts

 = Snuggles - Comforting or encouraging words or touch

*You can circle your favorite ideas!*

### Ideas:

 When you avoid emotions, they tend to stick around (what you resist persists).

 You can open to your emotional elephants in stages.

 Name it to tame it.

### Helpful Practices:

 Notice and name when you are resisting difficult feelings and activities.

 Find a way to name your feelings that works for you.

 Practice the four steps of opening to your elephants (noticing resistance, naming feelings, being curious, and offering kindness).

### Bonus Activity:

Make a fist with one hand (this is resistance), and with your other hand try to pry your fingers open. Does your fist get tighter or looser? Now instead of trying to force your fist open, gently hold the bottom of your fist. Does your fist loosen? Rather than fighting resistance, we can hold our resistance with mindfulness and compassion.

### Curiosity Question:

When do you hide your emotional elephants?

---

**A Note for Grown-Ups:**
In addition to encouraging children to talk about emotions, it's important to allow kids to open up over time. When a child is resisting acknowledging feelings, it can be helpful to gently inquire about the emotion, normalize how hard it can be to feel feelings, and invite the child to share about their emotions when they are ready (just like in the bonus activity above).

> Thank you for all of your help. I feel so grateful.

## Let's check off the ingredients we've gathered so far.

**Foundation Forest batter ingredients***

- [x] Eggs
- [ ] Flour
- [ ] Vanilla extract
- [ ] Baking powder
- [ ] Milk
- [ ] Butter

**Sweeteners from Sweet Meadow**

- [ ] Sugar
- [ ] Chocolate Chips
- [ ] Freeze dried strawberries
- [ ] Powdered sugar
- [ ] Honey

**Magic Potion from Magic Mountains**

Made from…. Rainbow, gems, heart energy, gold, and sprinkles

*Allergy friendly substitutes include flax seeds, gluten-free flour, and plant-based milk and oil.*

# We're crossing the bridge to Sweet Meadow!

# Adventures in Sweet Meadow!

What sweeteners do you like in your favorite desserts? Honey? Sugar? Maple syrup? In the case of resilience and self-compassion, our sweeteners include kindness, gratitude, and taking in positive experiences.

We have gathered the basic batter ingredients for our cake in Foundation Forest, so now we're off to Sweet Meadow to gather our sweeteners!

## *TREAT YOURSELF LIKE A GOOD FRIEND*

Are you ever hard on yourself like Anita was in the comic? This is really common. Kids (and grown-ups) are often harder on themselves than they are on others. Self-compassion invites us to treat ourselves like we would treat a good friend when things go wrong.

Have you ever noticed that some friends like a hug when they are upset and other friends don't even want you to know that something is wrong? Different friends like to be treated differently when they are struggling.

There's not one right way to be a good friend. In the same way, there are many different ways that we can be a good friend to ourselves.

Self-compassion can be comforting, like telling ourselves it's okay when we are having a hard time. Self-compassion can also help us be strong and do tough things. As we learn to be kinder to ourselves, we can also learn to be kinder to others.

Kindness grows kindness!

## Activity 7.1 How Would You Treat a Friend?

You can do this imagining exercise on your own and write your responses below, or you can do this exercise with a partner (maybe a grown-up?) and share your responses with each other.

**First imagine that a <u>friend of yours</u> is upset because they broke something special to them.**

If your friend told you that they were upset because they broke something special, what would you say to your friend? **Write down how you would respond to your friend.**

_____

_____

_____

_____

"When my friend ripped her hat, I told her I was sorry and I hoped she could fix it."
—Aarya, age 10

Sometimes I don't know what I should say to a friend.

Now, let's imagine that you are upset because you broke something special. What would you say to yourself? Would you be mad at yourself? **Write down what is true for you.**

_____

_____

_____

> I get upset with myself when I break something.

What differences are there between how you would treat a friend and how you would treat yourself (kindness, how big of a deal, how you feel, etc.)?

_____

_____

_____

"I use a harsh voice with myself and a soft voice with my friend."
—Anjali, age 10

"I have compassion for a friend, and I feel angry at myself."
—River, age 9

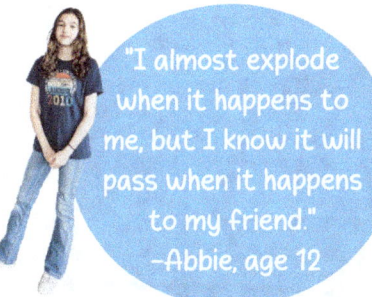

"I almost explode when it happens to me, but I know it will pass when it happens to my friend."
—Abbie, age 12

**Being self-compassionate means that we treat ourselves like a good friend when things go wrong.**

# Activity 7.2 Being a Good Friend

Sometimes we don't know what to say to our friends when they are upset, and different friends might like to hear different things. How might you respond in these situations?

If you like, you can draw or write another scenario:

What would you say to your friend?

**We are all learning how to be a good friend to others and to ourselves. Noticing how we would treat a friend can give us ideas about how we would like to treat ourselves.**

# Activity 7.3 Gentle and Strong Self-Compassion

When things go wrong, you may sometimes wish for gentle, comfortings words, and at other times you may wish for strong, encouraging words.

**Snuggles says comforting words, and Super Snuggles says encouraging words.**

Snuggles (gentle support)     Super Snuggles (strong support)

The phrases below include a mixture of strong and gentle words that some kids like.

**Put an "S" by the words that Snuggles would say.**
**Put an "SS" by the words that Super Snuggles would say.**

| | |
|---|---|
| SS You can do it! | That's hard! |
| S I'm sorry that happened. | I'm here for you. |
|    I believe in you. | That's frustrating. |
|    Would you like a hug? | Can I help you? |
|    You've got this! | What can I do? |
|    I understand. | It's okay. SS  S |
|    This won't last forever. | I love you. |
|    It's not your fault. | You're not alone. |
|    Other: _____ | Other: _____ |

*I think it sounds strong and gentle, so I'm putting S and SS.*

**Look at the last page and choose some of your favorite gentle and strong words.** Write words that feel comforting by the heart shaped leaves, and words that feel strong by the trunk of the tree.

**\*\*Try saying one of the words that you chose to yourself, and notice how it feels to treat yourself like a good friend.\*\***

# Activity 7.4 When Self-Compassion Feels Awkward

Some kids feel good when they say kind things to themselves, and other kids feel awkward. One reason it might feel strange at first is that we might not be used to saying kind things to ourselves.

At the bottom of the last activity (7.3), you were invited to try saying comforting and encouraging words to yourself. Did you say the kind words you chose to yourself?

☐ Yes
☐ No

If you haven't tried it yet, you can try it now!

"It feels peaceful to say the things that I like to hear."
–River, age 9

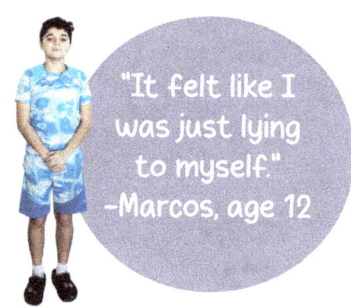
"It felt like I was just lying to myself."
–Marcos, age 12

Saying kind words to yourself might feel good, confusing, uncomfortable, or relaxing. Write down how you felt when you offered yourself kind words (or why you skipped that part of the activity)?

_____

_____

> Anytime we try something new, it can feel a little strange. Do you remember the first time you tried riding a bike? You might have felt wobbly and uncomfortable. Maybe part of you wanted to stop trying. But if you kept trying, you probably learned to ride the bike, and maybe you love riding your bike now. Can you remember an activity that you weren't sure about at first but now really like?

Notice how you feel when you try something new or different:

In this box, write your name with the hand you usually use.

In this box, write your name with your opposite hand.

How did it feel to write with your opposite hand?

_____

_____

Do you think if you practiced writing with your opposite hand everyday it would get easier?

☐ Yes
☐ No

Just like writing with your opposite hand, saying kind words to yourself can feel awkward at first. But if you keep practicing, it will feel good over time. Keep treating yourself like a good friend, and eventually you will have a friend inside of you. You will become your own best friend!

"When I'm doing something different, it feels kind of hard at first. But then when I keep practicing it gets so easy."
–River, age 9

Could I really be my own best friend?

# Adventure 7 Take-Aways

**Resilience Habit Animal**

 = Snuggles - Comforting or encouraging words or touch

*You can circle your favorite ideas!*

### Ideas and Practices:

 When you're struggling, ask yourself what you would say to a friend, and then say those words to yourself.

 You can use gentle words to comfort yourself and strong words to motivate yourself.

### Bonus Activity:

Start to notice how you treat others when they are struggling. Make a list of ideas for how you could treat yourself.

### Curiosity Question:

What words do you like to hear when things go wrong?

**A Note for Grown-Ups:**
Be sure to normalize resistance of down moments. While it's true that they are a part of living, sometimes kids and grown-ups need to vent because down moments can be frustrating!

**Trauma Sensitive Note:**

Self-kindness can be very challenging for some children (and grown-ups), especially those who have a strong inner critic or have experienced large amounts of adversity. It is important to be mindful of these challenges and allow children to open to self-kindness slowly.

**In our next adventure, we'll visit the Land of Kindness.**

"Kindness! My favorite! Kindness is so sweet."

"Oh! Like honey! I love honey!!"

## GROWING KINDNESS

Everyone wishes for good things in life—like friendship, freedom and happiness! What good things do you wish for?

In the comic, James sent kind wishes to his grandma and to himself. He wished for peace and love, but we can wish for anything, even happiness. We can send kind wishes to anyone at any time.

When we wish to be peaceful or happy, we are not trying to make these things happen. We are just planting seeds of kindness in our mind. These seeds can grow into good feelings and kind actions over time.

It's like you have a happiness plant in your mind. Sending kind wishes is like giving your plant water and sunshine so it can become tall and strong.

# Activity 8.1 Sending Kind Wishes

Let's try sending kind wishes!

Think about a person or animal that you care about. Who in your life makes you smile? This could be a little cousin, a grandparent, a teacher, a friend, or even a pet. It could be anyone!

What is the name of this person? _ _ _ _ _ _ _ _ _ _ _ _ _ _ _ _ _ _ _

 You can do the Kind Wishes practice on your own, or you can ask an adult to read it to you or help you listen to an audio recording at
https://jamielynntatera.com/workbook-for-kids-guided-practices/

We will wish for happiness, strength (like Super Snuggles), and that we can love and accept ourselves just as we are. But you can choose different words if you prefer.

### Kind Wishes

Begin by thinking of the person or animal you care about. If you like, you can close your eyes or look down while you picture in your mind this person or animal being happy.

Now you can send this person or animal some kind wishes. You can say each wish out loud, or repeat the wishes in your mind a couple of times.

- I wish for you to be happy.
- I wish for you to be strong.
- I wish for you to love and accept yourself as you are.

Now, you can picture yourself and this person or animal together. Maybe you are playing, maybe you are hugging each other or just standing next to each other. See if you can imagine the two of you happy together.
Now you can offer these kind wishes to both of you a couple of times.

- I wish for you and me to be happy.

- I wish for you and me to be strong.

- I wish for you and me to love and accept ourselves just as we are.

Now we are going to make our circle of kindness even bigger—offering kind wishes to yourself, the person or animal you care about, and everyone else. You can even include all of the animals if you would like.

- I wish for us all to be happy.

- I wish for us all to be strong.

- I wish for us all to begin to love and accept ourselves as we are.

Take a moment and notice how you feel. However you are feeling is okay (good, difficult, or mixed). If you closed your eyes, when you are ready, open your eyes.

Who did you like to send kind wishes to? You can choose more than one.

☐ The person you care about

☐ You and the person you care for

☐ Everyone (including you!)

How did the practice make you feel? Write or draw about your experience.

*This guided practice has been adapted from the Mindfulness and Self-Compassion for Children and Caregivers program.*

"It feels awkward to give myself kind wishes, but it feels great to give it to others."
—River, age 9

"When I give kind wishes, I feel peaceful and tired."
—Khalil, age 8

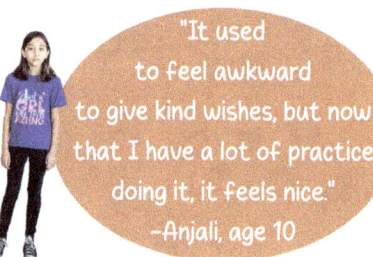
"It used to feel awkward to give kind wishes, but now that I have a lot of practice doing it, it feels nice."
—Anjali, age 10

# Activity 8.2 What Do You Value?

Below is a list of values and needs that we all share. Even though everyone needs these things, each person has their favorites. Circle your favorite values, and feel free to add your own! Think about what you might want to grow in your life.

(Circle your favorite values)

Rest  Space-to-be Me  Belonging  ORDER

Joy  Health  Peace

EASE  Self-acceptance

Play

Choice  GRATITUDE  Justice

Love  Kindness  Happiness

FRIENDSHIP  Respect

Safety  Creativity  STRENGTH

Meaning  Freedom  Humor

Other _____  Other _____

"I value humor because it makes everyone happier."
—Ambika, age 12

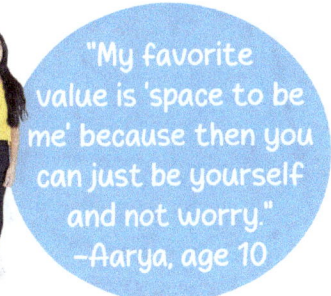

"My favorite value is 'space to be me' because then you can just be yourself and not worry."
—Aarya, age 10

# Activity 8.3 Make Your Own Kindness Shirt

What values did you circle in the last activity? Write three of your favorite values here. These can become your kind wishes.

1. _ _ _ _ _ _ _ _ _ _ _ _ _ _ _ _ _ _ _ _

2. _ _ _ _ _ _ _ _ _ _ _ _ _ _ _ _ _ _ _ _

3. _ _ _ _ _ _ _ _ _ _ _ _ _ _ _ _ _ _ _ _

You are a designer. You can create your own kindness t-shirts! Customize your shirt with your favorite values. "I wish for… or "I wish to be…." + your values. Don't forget to color them when you're done!

**You can offer yourself these kind wishes at any time!**

# Activity 8.4 Kindness for Everyone

Kindness is like the sun. There's more than enough sunlight and kindness for everyone!

Consider these questions: What good things (values) do you wish for others? Who can you wish these good things for?

Abbie from the Kids Team wishes for kindness and peace. She wrote her values in the center of the sun. She wishes for kindness and peace for her family and friends, and even people she doesn't know very well (including the man in the cafeteria).

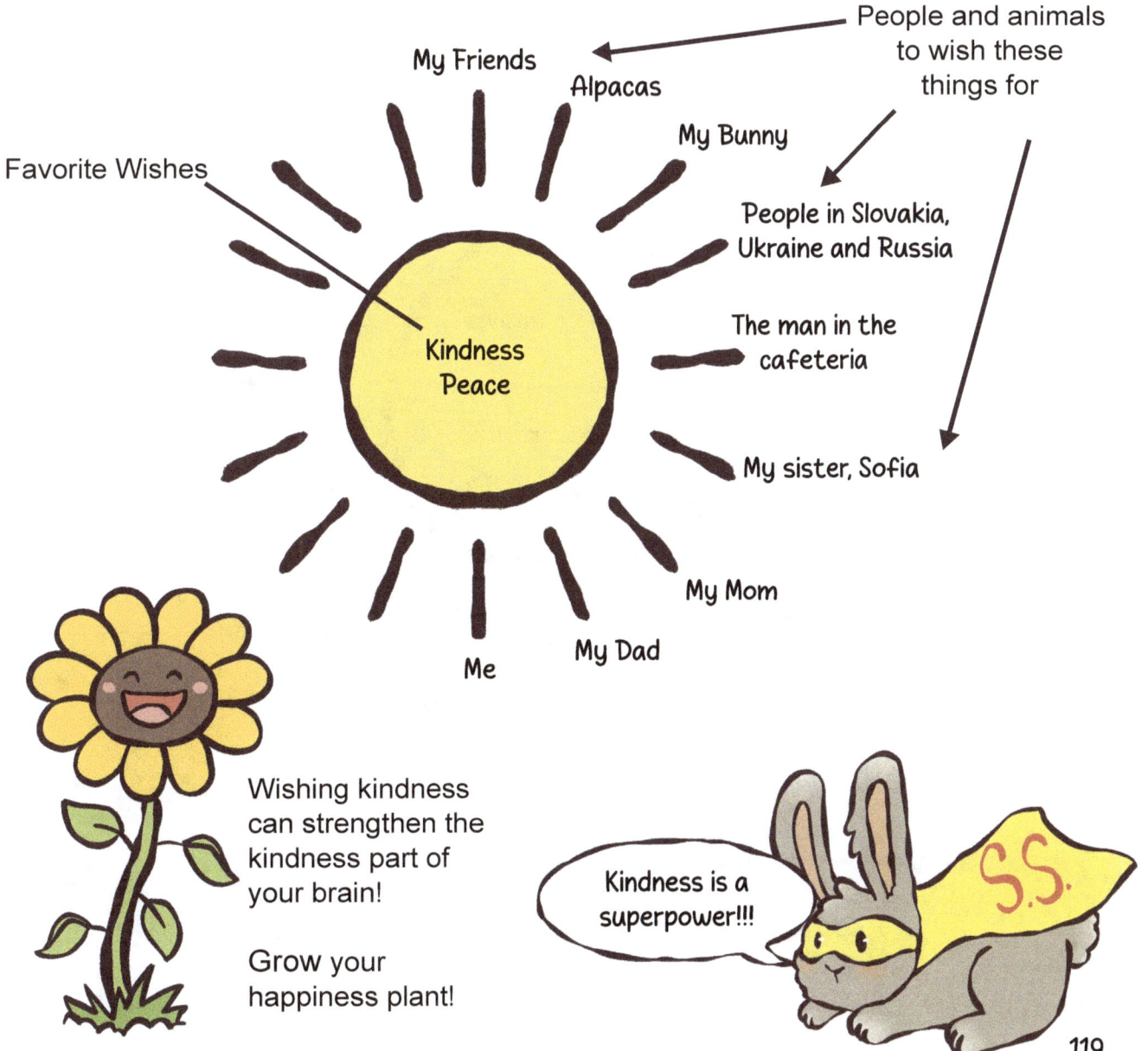

Wishing kindness can strengthen the kindness part of your brain!

Grow your happiness plant!

Now it's your turn.

Feel free to look back at the last page for ideas. You can make your circle of kindness as big as the whole world, even all the animals. And don't forget to include yourself!

**A Note for Grown-Ups:**
It can be powerful to create a custom kind wishes practice. Once children have found wishes they enjoy, you can create time each day (before bed can be great) to send and receive these wishes.

# Adventure 8 Take-Aways

**Resilience Habit Animals**

= Sunny - Thinking of good things

= Snuggles - Comforting or encouraging words or touch

*You can circle your favorite ideas!*

### Ideas:

 Sending kind wishes can strengthen the kindness part of our brain.

 We can send kind wishes to ourselves and others.

### Helpful Practices:

 Sending kind wishes to someone you like, yourself and everyone.

 Customized kind wishes (your own wishes).

### Bonus Activity:

You can write kind wishes on note cards or paint them on stones. You could scatter these throughout your house and read them whenever you want. If your parents say it's okay and can accompany you, you could even put notes or stones in places in your community.

### Curiosity Question:

Could you send a kind wish to someone who you don't like?

---

**A Note for Grown-Ups:**

Sending and receiving kind wishes (like peace or compassion) can be linked with your breathing. For example, you could offer peace to yourself when you breathe in, and send peace to others when you breathe out. This can be really useful to do when a child is struggling. When feeling empathy or frustration towards a child, you can breathe in compassion for yourself and then breathe out compassion for the child.

**Our adventures in Sweet Meadow will continue in book 2. See you in the Land of Sunshine!**

**Congratulations! You finished the adventures in the first Mindfulness and Self-Compassion Workbook for Kids! Be sure to celebrate!**

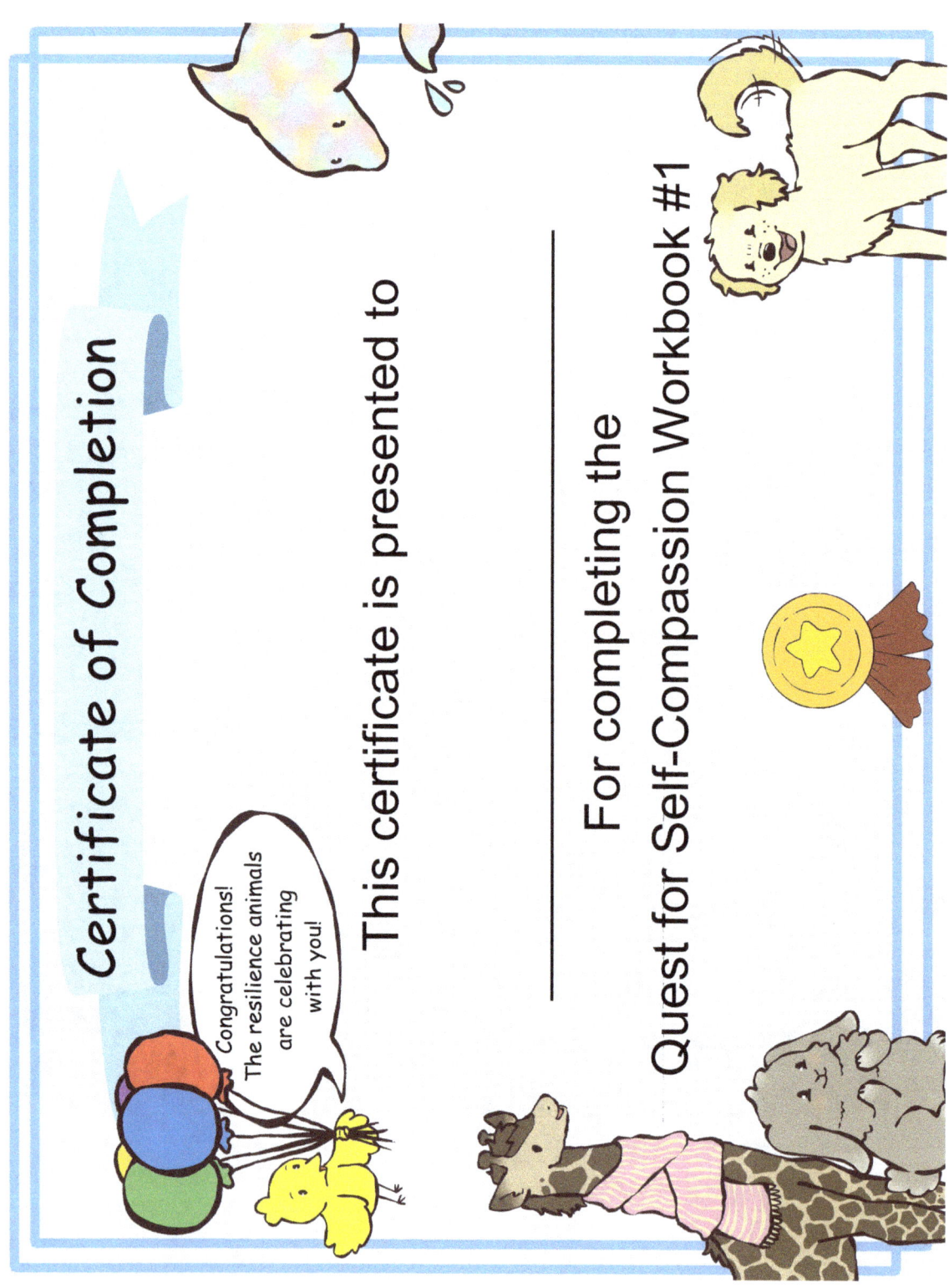

## …A SNEAK PEEK OF WORKBOOK 2
In our first adventure, we'll visit the Land of Sunshine and meet Flame the Dragon.

## Acknowledgments:

This series of activity books would not be possible without the people who created self-compassion training for adults and teens. Thank you to Christopher Germer and Kristin Neff for sharing the Mindful Self-Compassion program with me and gifting me with the resource of self-compassion. Thank you to Karen Bluth for inspiring me to teach the Mindful Self-Compassion for Teens program, and igniting curiosity in me for how I could share self-compassion with kids.

Thank you to my own children - Maya and Anjali - for allowing me to experiment and talk endlessly about mindfulness and self-compassion! And thank you to Patrick Bieser for taking care of the kids and washing dishes while I sat at the computer writing this book.

Thank you to the Kids Team - especially the original six members: Anjali, Ambika, Aarya, Abbie, Sofia, and Maya (and Lailah for the quest idea). Your feedback and creative ideas have made this workbook what it is! Thank you Alexis Warshall for bringing the illustration ideas to life, and thanks to Alyssa Brown for detailed formatting!

Thank you to the many friends who have supported me in sharing and refining my ideas over the years, including Miska Barrett, Anvita Mishra, and Mary Novotny. Your support means so much to me.

Truly, I couldn't have done it without all of you. We did it together!

And I'm so grateful to each and every one of you who purchased this book. Thank you for caring about children and helping them grow self-compassion. I wrote this book so that children don't have to suffer like I did when I was young. If you found this book helpful, please give it a review on Amazon or another platform. Your review can help others discover this book so children suffer less.

## Resources:

Free companion Masterclass with Jamie Lynn on How to Help Kids with Tricky Thoughts and Feelings using the Mindfulness and Self-Compassion Workbook for Kids:
https://jamielynntatera.com/workbook-for-kids-resources

Jamie Lynn offers a wealth of resources in her newsletter, podcast, blog, YouTube, and social media: https://linktr.ee/jamielynntatera

Parent-Child Mindfulness and Self-Compassion class (kids ages 7-11 with their parent/grown-up):
https://jamielynntatera.com/parent-child-self-compassion-class/

Dr. Kristin Neff has a wealth of information about self-compassion on her website: https://self-compassion.org/

Grow your own resilience resources in Jamie Lynn's Resilience Habits for Parents course: https://jamielynntatera.com/resilience-habits-for-parents/

### Train to Teach Mindfulness and Self-Compassion to Kids:

Train to teach resilience and self-compassion to children:
https://jamielynntatera.com/train-to-teach/

## References:

Germer, C., & Neff, K. (2018). *The Mindful Self-Compassion Workbook: A Proven Way to Accept Yourself, Build Inner Strength, and Thrive.* New York: Guilford Press.

Germer, C., & Neff, K. (2019). *Teaching the Mindful Self-Compassion Program: A Guide for Professionals.* New York: Harper Collins.

Tatera, J. (2020). Teacher Guide for the Mindfulness and Self-Compassion for Children and Caregivers Program (available for trained Mindfulness and Self-Compassion for Children and Caregivers teachers).

Tatera, J. (2020). *The Path to Resilience Photo Book.* Milwaukee, WI: Wholly Mindful, LLC.

## About the Author:

Jamie Lynn Tatera is passionate about helping kids and grown-ups learn resilience and self-compassion skills. She is an elementary school educator, a certified Mindful Self-Compassion teacher, and the creator of the Mindfulness and Self-Compassion for Children and Caregivers (MSC-CC) program, which is a parent-child adaptation of the Mindful Self-Compassion course. She trains parents, educators and clinicians in her resiliency programs: https://jamielynntatera.com.

Jamie Lynn lives in Shorewood, Wisconsin, with her husband and two daughters, Maya and Anjali. When Jamie Lynn is not writing and teaching, she enjoys dancing, doing yoga, and spending time in nature.

## About the Illustrator:

Alexis Warshall is a MIAD graduate who loves creating fun and whimsical art. She loves spending time outside with nature and her animals.

www.ingramcontent.com/pod-product-compliance
Lightning Source LLC
Chambersburg PA
CBHW081430070526
44586CB00020B/2536